NOT DEAD

The Case for Tanks in the Modern Battlespace

NOT DEAD

The Case for Tanks in the Modern Battlespace

by

Charles S. Oliviero

The reports of my death have been exaggerated.

Mark Twain, 1897

Library and Archives Canada Cataloguing in Publication
Oliviero, Charles S., author
Not Dead: The Case for Tanks in the Modern Battlespace/Charles S. Oliviero

Issued in print and electronic formats.
ISBN: 978-1-998501-74-8 (paperback)
ISBN: 978-1-998501-75-5 (ebook)

Editor: Phil Halton
Cover Design: Pablo Javier Herrera
Interior Design: Winston S. Prescott

Double Dagger Books Ltd.
Toronto, Ontario, Canada
www.doubledagger.ca

TABLE OF CONTENTS

PREFACE

This short volume on tanks and armoured warfare grew out of a lecture I gave at the Royal United Services Institute of Vancouver Island (RUSI VI) back in December 2024.[1] The lecture was a response to the question "Is the tank dead?" and I proceeded to explain to my audience, most of whom were not ex-army, why the quip from Mark Twain in the 19th century was appropriate to what they were reading in the press and hearing from an entire pack of earnest but ill-informed journalists and pundits.

I will admit that I was quite strident in my denunciation of the various claims, convinced as I remain, that too much of what passes for journalism in the current media sphere is meant not so much to educate and inform as it is to shock and agitate. To quote the late Senator from New York the inimitable Daniel Patrick Moynihan, who famously said, "You're entitled to your own opinions, but not your own facts," too much uninformed opinion is being pass off as truth. My lecture was well-received, and I was pleased to obtain much positive feedback. RUSI VI has a habit of posting all lectures on their web page and after that occurred, I began to get feedback from further afield. As with previous opinions that I have published,

---

[1] *Here is the link to the original lecture and slides: https://rusiviccda.org/is-the-king-of-battle-the-main-battle-tank-obsolete/*

my old high school friend and classmate Angelo Mattacchione contacted me and just as he had done when prompting me to write my short book on leadership, *Tactical Jazz*, Angelo suggested that I consider transforming my lecture into a short book. As a graduate and professional engineer, he was fascinated by the technical aspects of the tank as presented in the lecture. As a husband, father, and grandfather he was interested in the human dimension of what I had said in the lecture, and pressed me to explain more fully all of these aspects for a wider audience.

As I usually did when we sat together in high school, I appreciated Angelo's advice — and I took it. This book is the result.

ABOVE: *American Sherman tank advances in Italy, 1944.*

FOREWORD

There was a strange dinosaurian quality about the first tanks; huge metal rhomboids, trimmed with tracks, that came lumbering and clanking out of the mist. Winston Churchill is said to have given the new war machines the name "tanks" in order to obscure their real purpose; armed and armoured vehicles designed to restore some element of movement on the Western Front during the latter half of World War One. As it was, whole armies had become immobilized by the lethal technological balance between the offence and the defence. The generals on both sides were strategically bankrupt. Their solution was simply to pour more and more men into the insatiable maw.

Now, for the first time, a small number of soldiers were able to shelter in the lee of iconic tanks like Little Willie. This was, of course, an unbelievably sensible thing to do, but what it presaged was something vitally important to Dr. Oliviero's superb analysis of tanks and tank warfare, namely the evolution of combined arms warfare. Soon, those same soldiers would find themselves killing enemy tanks and paving the way for their own.

What Little Willie and other tanks of that era lacked was speed. Indeed, they moved at only two miles an hour, slower than a soldier walked! However, there was a tiny coterie of military thinkers, during the interwar period, who realized the full potential of the tank; men like the German, Erich von Manstein, the Frenchman, Charles de Gaulle, and the Englishman, JFC Fuller. They appreciated the enormous potential of mechanization (although some French military planners were still considering the formation of cavalry regiments in 1938) and the need to harvest the advantages of shock derived from massive high speed tank attacks.

These calculations, buttressed by colossal production quotas, resulted in huge tank battles in World War Two with hundreds of tanks clashing in brutal, bloody, and prolonged encounters. All of the combatants had to wrestle with the complex compromises involved in tank design, balancing firepower, weight and mobility. If, for example, you wanted your tank to go faster you needed a bigger engine which added to the machine's overall weight and reduced the interior storage space for ammunition; and so on, and so forth. Any change in one of the three elements immediately affected the other two.

And then there was the central problem; how best to deploy your forces? How best to undertake reconnaissance, how best to exploit the terrain to your advantage, how to ensure adequate logistical support, and how best to blend your forces to achieve the greatest possible effect? As a one-time naval navigator, I was fascinated by the similarities between warships manoeuvring on the ocean and tanks moving across the desert in engagements like El Alamein (1942) and the Battle of 73 Easting (1991) in the Iraqi desert. In the latter, the coalition forces lost one tank; the Iraqis lost 160!

Dr. Oliviero has written a splendid introduction to tank warfare. He had a full career as a Canadian tank commander, completed his doctorate in military studies, has written extensively on strategy, tactics, and combat, and lectures internationally. He accompanies us into the little known world of tank warfare; revealing the strengths and weaknesses of prevailing doctrine, the challenges of hitting the enemy at 1,000 yards when your tank is hurtling across the landscape at 45 miles an hour, and the artistry of such encounters when undertaken by a deeply experienced tank commander.

Professor James Boutilier, PhD
Victoria, British Columbia

INTRODUCTION

Mark Twain's 1897 quip to a *New York Journal* reporter was obviously meant to be funny, but it makes an important point. Journalists are often wrong. It's been more than a century since Twain spoke to that reporter, and we now live in a world where information can be found at the touch of a screen or by asking a digital assistant, and yet there are strong indications that we are now *less* well informed than when newspapers ruled the media landscape.

There's been considerable speculation in the media recently on the usefulness of tanks in modern warfare. Have drones made them obsolete? Has the nature of war changed forever thereby making the tank irrelevant? Is the tank dead?

Based on what they've seen happening in Ukraine, journalists with little or no knowledge of modern mechanized warfare have made bold statements. The statements may make good headlines and "click bait" online, but few of the assertions are based on solid analyses. These claims are not conclusions, they are uninformed exclamations based on what is *perceived* — and perceived by amateurs — when it comes to warfighting in general and to tanks in particular.

Consider a mundane example. The average person watching someone solving a Rubik's Cube in a matter of seconds — even in slow motion — can barely understand how the solution is found. It all happens so fast, and without deep knowledge of how to solve the puzzle, it all seems like luck, or perhaps even magic. But to an advanced "cuber" the moves quickly indicate whether the solver is an expert or just lucky.

In the cognitive sciences, this is called the "expert/novice divide". Experts can glimpse a situation and see something completely different from someone who is new to the subject. This divide is true in practically every domain. Modern mechanized warfare is not an occupation for amateurs and paying too much heed to pundits who know little about military theory, mechanized warfare, or tank warfare, can quickly teach the wrong lessons.

Tanks have an enduring visual allure and therefore get more attention than they rightly deserve. A quick scan of any major news story proves my point. Whenever the media wants an eye-catching visual for a military story, there is inevitably a picture of a tank. I spent my professional life — both in uniform and in academe — studying mechanized warfare from both the theoretical and the practical aspects. I commanded an Armoured Reconnaissance (Armoured Recce) troop, a tank squadron, an Armoured Cavalry (Armoured Cav) regiment that had both Main Battle Tanks (MBTS) and Armoured Recce, and briefly even commanded a *Bundeswehr* tank brigade (*10. Panzerbrigade* had about 95 Leopard IIs) on a major European field exercise. I've trained and educated many hundreds of soldiers, non-commissioned officers and officers in modern warfare, specifically focused on the employment of armoured forces, whether they were tanks, Armoured Recce, or Armoured Cav.

Modern tanks are the thoroughbreds of mechanized warfare, and they are devastatingly effective when "ridden" correctly. Conversely, they are giant targets when misemployed, as the Russian Army has repeatedly demonstrated so dramatically in Ukraine.

But you need to know what you're watching and what it means. Watching a drone or tank engaging another tank is not like watching a tennis match. Just because it appears straightforward, doesn't mean that it is. There's much more going on than may be obvious to an uninformed observer.

Here's an oversimple analogy: Giving a peasant two racehorses and then wondering why the horses died after spending only a couple of days pulling plows is not evidence that horses can't pull plows. You need to understand the environment, the situation, the terrain, the horses, and the plows. To quote one of my instructors when I was a young officer candidate, "Remember, sir, *misuse* is *abuse*." To put it another way, using a piece of equipment improperly is worse than not using it at all. Much of what has led to the declaration of tanks being obsolete has been based on observing such improper use, and if the observer doesn't know that it's improper, then the wrong conclusion may be easily formed.

The question of the viability of the tank is about much more than an issue of bad or outdated tactics. It's about expertise. It's about depth of understanding. As Aristotle famously said, "Those who know, do. Those who understand, teach." In a nutshell, that is why I wrote this book. Not surprisingly, the general public is blissfully ignorant of tank warfare, and in a peace-loving liberal democracy, that is not a bad thing. But interest in mechanized warfare remains enduringly high and learning enough to know when the media is wrong, is one of the duties of an informed citizenry.

Employing armoured forces in general, and tanks in particular, requires a highly specialized set of skills and a deep knowledge of everything from physics to psychology to mathematical probability. Gathering this knowledge and expertise begins as a science and grows into an art form (albeit a deadly art form) as one progresses in skill and comprehension. It takes time, study, and practice, but if one doesn't get the science right the second stage, the art, never gets practised. To quote Aristotle again, "Education is bitter, but the fruit is sweet."

So why this book? First, to educate the general public on tanks, to help the lay reader. As I said above, there is an enduring interest in tanks but most volumes on the subject gloss over the fundamentals. This volume starts there, with the fundamentals. Second, this book seeks to correct the many misunderstandings that exist on the employment of tanks, whatever their configuration.

In order to achieve these two goals, we'll need to begin at a theoretical level. We need to begin by putting aside hyperbole and appreciating that the *nature* of war remains constant even as the *character* of war changes daily. The nature of war is violence. How that violence is controlled, or unleashed, pertains to the character of war. And that character changes routinely as new tools and methods are developed and then employed. This distinction is not trivial. It's fundamental to understanding war, warfare, and its many aspects. It's important to our topic here because although technology has increased the risks to tanks, that same technology has made tanks more effective and lethal.

To the uninformed, this interplay with constant *nature* and changing *character* may seem paradoxical. It isn't as long as one keeps this simple thought fixed in one's mind:

War's nature is constant; war's character is changing.

Thus, every new tactic, every advance in technology, and every new technique has an effect on warfare, on how we fight. But it does not change the nature of war. Keeping this fact fixed in our minds helps us to understand what we are observing, which in the case of the viability of tanks is nothing more than an advancement of technology and *not* a change in the nature of war.

The use of drones is a perfect case in point. The drone has not changed war, and it really has only barely changed warfare. Watching a ten-dollar drone drop a grenade into the open hatch of a multimillion-dollar tank may seem like the best example of why the tank is obsolete, but there is nothing new in that. It's no different than watching an untrained peasant impale a highly trained soldier — equipped with the latest weapons — with a piece of sharpened bamboo. It's a snapshot of the endless give and take of arms races, and the ever-evolving character of warfare.

The claim of the tank's demise is neither unique nor new, and neither is it restricted to land warfare. The invention of heavier-than-air aircraft did not make land forces obsolete, as was predicted in 1921 by Giulio Douhet, the father of airpower theory. The use of submarines did not remove the need for surface warships as has been routinely predicted in every major conflict of the 19th and 20th (and 21st) centuries. Machine guns did not make infantry obsolete … The list is nearly endless, and the claims are breathtaking — and breathtakingly mistaken.

OUTLINE

The thesis of this book is straightforward: Not only is the tank not obsolete, it remains land warfare's single most potent weapon.

In order to demonstrate the thesis, the argument is divided into three parts.

Part I sets the stage. It provides some background, explains some of the often-confusing terminology, as well as offering some insights (and warnings) in order to prepare the reader for the central issue — the art and science of tank employment in Part II.

Part II discusses the employment of armoured vehicles in general, and specifically focuses on the employment of tanks, including some hands-on examples of how to employ them correctly.

Part III offers some battlespace exemplars.

The book then ends with some brief conclusions.

Finally, I have included three short annexes that are germane to the subject of tank warfare but are distinct from the thesis that tanks remain relevant to the modern battlespace.

This short endeavour is not an attempt to cover all aspects of tank warfare. That would take volumes and thousands of hours. It's a modest attempt to offer the interested observer a better basis upon which to make up their own mind when next they hear that tanks are a waste of time, money, and resources. The title says it all: *NOT DEAD*.

PHILOSOPHY

Before proceeding, it's important for the reader to understand what underpins my thinking. This book is not about doctrine. The thoughts found here are my own and based on my personal experiences and studies. Some of my thoughts don't align well with official doctrine. During my career, I frequently was accused of being a heretic, and to be honest, that may have been fair criticism. It was my habit to question everything, including doctrine, and often this habit made those around me uncomfortable.

But I believe that discomfort and the questioning of how things are done is a good thing. Only by questioning can we learn and only by learning can we grow to understand what we are doing. It may be an imperfect methodology, but it is what I do, and it has worked for me.

In my previous books (*Praxis Tacticum*, *Strategia*, *The Birth of Enlightened Command*, *Tactical Jazz*, and *Dangerous Lessons*, and even my military adventure novel *The Cohort*) I've frequently taken a philosophical approach to my arguments, wanting my readers to think deeply about the case presented. In this book, I've modified that methodology somewhat. Here I look to be more practical and more explanatory. I'm writing here for the young soldier just learning the profession of arms, for any general student of war and warfare, and for the average person with a general interest in military affairs, war, warfare, and of course, the modern main battle tank.

To borrow the motto of the 11ᵗʰ Armored Cavalry Regiment, the US Army's storied "Blackhorse Regiment" — *Allons!*

PART I: FOUNDATIONS

BACKGROUND

Since this book is intended for both the general reader and someone with some knowledge of armoured vehicles, I'll begin with some definitions, roles, characteristics, vulnerabilities, and limitations of armoured warfare and its various components. This will establish the base for explanations that follow in the remainder of the book, particularly for the readers who are newcomers to the subject.

KEY DEFINITIONS

Note: When considering the four key definitions below, remember that it's important to distinguish between a weapons system and its employment. In other words, what it is versus how it's used.

Armour: This is the generic term for all armoured vehicles but in the common military vernacular it's most often used as a synonym for "tanks", and it can be confusing. All professions have their own jargon, and it often changes by country. Thus, when military personnel talk about employing armour, they could be talking about the protection they are adding to a vehicle or a location, but what they are normally referring to are main battle tanks (MBTs). Like all jargon, it's imperfect, so keep it in mind that when discussing "armour", context is key.

Armoured Recce: This is the generic term for all armoured reconnaissance.

Otherwise stated, finding out what is going on by using soldiers in vehicles. It can involve practically any and all armoured fighting vehicles (AFVs) in just about any combination of forces. It's important to appreciate that recce is a function carried out by all forces in the battlespace, both purposefully and also as a matter of normal routine reporting. There are many types of recce. All units in the battlespace perform close combat recce, some conduct aerial recce, and some conduct signals recce. Gathering information is a constant and multifaceted task for everyone. But the term Armoured Recce is specifically used to refer to specially trained, mounted troops doing specialized tasks.

Sometimes it can even be confusing for military people. For instance, a Canadian mechanized infantry battalion has an integral battalion recce platoon and on occasion, they will be in the same or similar vehicles to the armour regiment's regimental recce troop. The two groups may look the same and even be given similar tasks, but their skills and training have only minimal overlap. Recall what I said about jargon.

Armoured Cavalry: This term is at once ill-defined and widely used. For decades, it remained primarily within the US Army, although the Royal Australian Armoured Corps also used it. Today it's more common, but even more confusing because different militaries use the term to mean different things. In this book I do my best to keep it generic.

The simplest way to look at Armoured Cav is as a multi-purpose armoured unit that's capable of a wide range of missions, but whose *primary* role is recce. The key difference between Armoured Cav and Armoured Recce is not equipment; it is *mindset*. Irrespective of how they are equipped, Armoured Cav soldiers are trained to fight for information if necessary, (sometimes referred to as "recce by fire") whereas Armoured Recce does not seek combat *per se*. Like all army units, it's capable of fighting, but because it's usually a light force. Armoured Recce prefers to seek information without having to fight for it, whereas Armoured Cav can fight for information if it must — "sneak and peek" vs "recce by fire." This distinction will be discussed later in greater detail, but it's important to keep in mind that Armoured Cav and Armoured Recce may be very similar, but they are *not* the same.

MBT: This term is the easiest to define for our purposes here. It describes the class of tanks that are designed for direct fire combat. In the whole family of AFVs there is a wide range of tanks designed for a series of diverse functions, but all MBTs are designed and employed with a single focus: engage the enemy *directly*. Thus, all MBTs are tanks, but all tanks are not MBTs.

Summary. Using armour of any type is based on a single overriding purpose: The need to build combat power. Whether we are discussing, armour generically, MBTs, Armoured Recce or Armoured Cav, their use always stems from the single greatest decision-driver for all military commanders, namely, the need to build combat power.

SIMPLE VS CORRECT

In order to follow some of the distinctions I'm about to make, it's necessary to take a step back and investigate how we teach and learn certain subjects.

Frequently, we opt for the simplicity of a comfortable solution over the complication of a correct one. Or, as John F. Kennedy put it "too often we enjoy the comfort of opinion without the discomfort of thought." Frequently it's not even a conscious act. There's little point in trying to explain to a young child that a ball bounces because of the laws of physics, but by the time we describe it to high school students it must be about physics.

I'll describe some examples before proceeding specifically to armoured warfare. I do this in order to set the scene for my argument that just because something is widely accepted, doesn't necessarily mean that it's correct. To be clear, I'm not accusing anyone of intentional distortion. I'm arguing that there's often a broad misunderstanding, and if that misunderstanding becomes common, it eventually is treated as truth.

First, we need to recognize the difference between what's true and what's correct. Truth is *factual* whereas correctness is *normative*. Otherwise stated, truth can be objectively tested whereas correctness is usually based on what is good, desirable, or permissible as defined by someone or some group.

UNIVERSAL TRUTHS

Water boils at 100°C — unless there are impurities in it, it's under pressure, or it's at altitude. The boiling point of water is dependent upon many things. Thus, the statement is *true* but not always *correct*.

The sun always rises in the east — except at the poles, where the concept of east and west breaks down. Again, the statement is *true* but not always *correct*.

Sharks must keep swimming to survive — except some species can pump water over their gills while resting, and some sharks have learned to sleep with their mouths open in underwater currents. *True* but not always *correct*.

TANK EXAMPLE

One of the reasons that some pundits believe that the tank is no longer viable is because of a simple error: we confuse the weapon with its employment. The tank is the weapon; how we use it (or misuse it) is a completely different matter. Let's investigate why.

In the Royal Canadian Armoured Corps, as well as other armies, we have lived with a similar comfortable simplicity that has led to the improper employment of tanks, but the reasons for this vary.

Most people, including military historians, are unaware that the most successful tank ace on the Allied side in World War II was a Canadian. In fact, he was a highly decorated, and respected member of my own regiment. The Allies' top tank ace was Major Sydney Valpy Radley-Walters. "Rad" as he was called, went on to command my regiment and retired as a brigadier general.

I had the good fortune of spending time with General Rad throughout my career, and when I commanded the regiment, he was a great source of advice and support. His enduring lesson to all of us was that best tank killer was another tank.

Rad came to be the proponent of this "tank vs tank" argument for all the right reasons. He didn't win a Military Cross or become the Allied tank ace by accident. When he fought his way onto the beaches of Normandy and into the heart of Germany, the best tank killer then was indeed another tank. The "Firefly" version of the Canadian Sherman tank was our best hope at destroying German panzers and Rad internalized that truth. For the remainder of his career, he never gave it up.

Generations of Canadian armour officers have taken Rad's words as gospel and continue to do so. What's the best tank killer? Strictly speaking, it remains another tank due to its accuracy, speed of fire, range of ammunition, and the adage that it takes a thief to catch a thief. So, like so many examples, it's *true*, it just isn't *correct*.

Tanks are far more valuable using their immense combat power to focus on other things like hunting down headquarters or supply depots, exactly as British Major General JFC Fuller insisted a *century* ago, but our belief that the tank is a tank-killer has led many commanders — irrespective of their branch — to misemploy tanks primarily as tank killers. This is akin to using a pipe wrench as a hammer. It may work, but it is an improper utilization of a tool designed for other things. As my friend Lieutenant Colonel Steve Moffat put it so well, "We've been doing it wrong for so long that it feels right."

This misemployment of tanks stems from the common human failing of not fully investigating why something is done the way it is. In 1711, Alexander Pope, an English poet and essayist of the Enlightenment wrote a highly influential poem (*An Essay on Criticism*), which gave us several lines that we use to this day including *To err is human; to forgive, divine*, and *A little learning is a dang'rous thing; Drink deep, or taste not the Pierian Spring*. It's this last comment that's important to us here.

His reference to the mythical Pierian Spring, which represented a divine source of knowledge, inspiration, and enlightenment is meant to warn of the need for a deep understanding of whatever is being considered instead of just a passing knowledge. With only a shallow understanding of any topic, there is great potential for misunderstanding — and that is where we are with the employment of tanks in modern warfare.

For the time being, all I ask is that you accept that the vast array of anti-tank weapons used by the infantry and close support aviation are the best tank killers — if not technically, then at least tactically. By the end of the book, I hope that you'll understand why is this both *true* and *correct*.

COMBAT POWER

The whole purpose of any weapon system is to build combat power. We need to discuss this foundational notion because without understanding the fundamental premise of combat power, nothing else matters in this investigation of tanks.

The concept of combat power is the commander's focal point because everything in the tactical realm must be seen through this lens. In combat, the commander has a single aim: win the engagement. In order to do so, he must not only conceptualize, but also master, the idea of combat power. How to build it; how to employ it; how to concentrate it. Critically, nothing in mechanized warfare builds combat power like a tank.

It should come as no surprise that every army has a slightly different way of considering combat power. Most take a very mechanistic view, with almost formulaic explanations of how to build or employ it. They define it in terms of its various components and elements, which are frequently referred to as combat functions, and how to combine them. Some doctrine says that there are four functions, some say six, some say even more. Irrespective of how many components, parts, elements, or building blocks there are success lies in knowing two things:

1. How to combine the combat functions in order to build combat power, and
2. How to employ that power correctly.

Let's begin by looking at some of these building blocks. The more obvious ones are leadership, firepower, information, movement, logistics, communications, and protection.

Clearly, there are other elements, which could be considered but my intent here is not to break down the concept in a way that doctrinal manuals tend to do. If you are the type of person that learns best from that approach, then doctrinal manuals and their mechanistic reductionism may be a good choice for you. Personally, I prefer to consider this issue conceptually or holistically.

Since war is a human endeavour, humans guide all of the weapons and tactical decisions. Whatever the force or the mission, human minds lie at the core of the combat power being built. If you can destroy or disrupt the hundreds, even thousands, of tiny human actions and linkages that combine to create your enemy's combat power, you will win — irrespective of how much carnage you actually create. So, using tanks, alongside all of the other weapons at their disposal, commanders use a dynamic and skilful combination of movement, firepower, protection and leadership, *et al* to create, and then employ, destructive force, i.e. combat power.

Thus, it's less about the specific tools, and more about how those tools are combined and employed. Remember, what I said earlier: Don't confuse the weapon with its employment.

COMBINED ARMS THEORY

Combined arms theory is the core principle of all conventional modern warfare. It demands the integration of the different combat arms (infantry, armour, artillery, combat engineers, and tactical aviation) to achieve a synergistic effect, where the whole is *greater* than the *sum* of its parts. Achieving synergy maximizes strengths and mitigates weaknesses. Consequently, this synergy creates more combat power than if the forces were employed independently or in a consecutive sequence. Think of a human hand. The power of a fist is easily more that five times that of any single finger.

This theory forms the foundation of most armies' military doctrine, and any differences among them lie less in theory and more in application. The theory maintains that it's practically impossible to build maximum combat power unless the various arms are combined into a single fighting formation under a unified command. The premise is a simple one. Individual arms should not fight alone. Only by combining with other arms to form a combined arms team, can a commander efficiently build maximal combat power.

Why? The strength of each individual arm covers the weakness of the other arms in a synergistic way. Thus, the vulnerability of infantry to direct fire is covered by armour; the vulnerability of armour to dismounted infantry is covered by infantry; engineers provide mobility and counter-mobility; artillery provides an "umbrella" of indirect fire and so on.

Irrespective of who first derived combined arms theory (Prussia or the USSR), no one has practised *Gefecht der verbundenen Waffen* (combined arms combat), nor insisted upon its near-evangelical application, longer than the Germans. But theory is one thing, and application is another. Embracing the theory is not proof that it can be used. The proof of the pudding, as we say, is in the eating. In this case, whether a commander can skilfully combine (and recombine) movement, firepower, protection and leadership, to build the destructive force of combat power.

In summary, although combined arms combat can mean different things to different people, at its heart it encompasses three vital essentials:

1. Independent arms and weapons systems must be systematically combined in order to both maximize the strengths as well as minimize the weaknesses of each individual arm or weapon system;
2. Combined arms teams work together under a single commander; and
3. The tactics and drills used by a combined arms team are not distinct from those used by each arm separately. Simply put, forces don't modify how they fight because they have merged with others to operate as part of a greater combined arms effort.

INTERIM CONCLUSIONS

This completes our quick tour of a series of some foundational concepts and practices in order to set the stage. We've established some common definitions, and drawn a critical distinction between what is factual and what is normative through the use of simple examples. Last, we had a short, sharp review of combat power and combined arms theory.

We are now equipped to move on to the realm of armoured warfare in general and MBTs in particular.

The higher the concentration of tanks, the faster, greater, and more sweeping will be the success — and the smaller our own losses.

Panzer General Heinz Guderian, 1940

PART II: THE ART AND SCIENCE OF TANK EMPLOYMENT

INTRODUCTION

The proper employment of armoured forces requires a highly specialized set of skills along with a deep knowledge of everything from physics to mathematical probability. Gathering this knowledge and expertise begins as a science and grows into an art form as one progresses in skill and comprehension. In that vein, let's begin with the science of tank design after which we'll move to tank characteristics, and then close with the employment of armoured forces.

DESIGN

In order to incorporate the deadly capabilities we have been considering, we must appreciate that modern tank design is a delicately balanced compromise of three dynamic parameters:

1. Firepower;
2. Mobility; and
3. Protection.

Interestingly, although these three parameters are universally accepted, they are not universally applied. Each country, based on its doctrine, military culture, and national way of war, places its emphasis on different parameters. The British and Israelis traditionally emphasize protection, whereas the Germans have always emphasized mobility and the Americans have leaned towards firepower. Since we are not investigating particular vehicles or countries, we will look at this issue generically.

Like the old joke about being able to do a job well, do it quickly, or do it cheaply, but not being able to do all three, the three design parameters interact in the same way. Every tank design is necessarily a balance of these parameters and all three cannot be priorities.

Firepower

Arguably, this parameter is the most important since the whole point of having such a massive weapon is to be able to use its gun. But having the largest, most accurate cannon does not come unconstrained. It comes with many secondary and tertiary considerations. Large-caliber ammunition is heavy, bulky and depending on the type and design (ammunition can be one-piece or two-piece), it must be handled, stored and loaded differently.

The physical size of the gun itself is also an issue. The larger the caliber, the heavier the barrel as well as the breach block assembly, and frequently the longer the barrel needs to be. All of these design issues affect not just the weight and the dimensions of the vehicle, but also determine the amount of horsepower required to move it, which can have an impact on the fuel type and even constrain simple considerations like the vehicular center of gravity, its height, weight and balance characteristics. All of these considerations make tank design highly complex. Last, will the barrel be rifled or smooth bore? It may seem like an inane question, but the answer affects all sorts of things like the ammunition types, the fire control system, resupply requirements, and even the crew size. In short, the larger the caliber of the main armament, the greater the competition for internal working and storage space.

Mobility

I'll refrain from entering the swamp of the tracks versus wheels debate, which continues to rage since fundamentally, all tanks are tracked vehicles. This parameter is tied directly to agility and has some not-so-obvious components. Let me go on the record as not being a fan of large, wheeled, AFVs.

Since tracks are a given (trust me on this), then the issue moves to what type of track, how wide it needs to be, and what materials will be used. A friend and regimental brother spent a year at the British Royal Armoured Corps Training Regiment and graduated with a Master of Science degree. His thesis project? A tank track pin. Not as simple as just grabbing a steel rod. Clearly, the design of tank tracks considers important factors like ground pressure, maintenance, durability, suspension, and speed — both on hard surfaces and cross-country.

Last, we need to consider the obvious: How much horsepower will the tank need in order to allow it to accelerate quickly, maintain high speeds, and move with agility across different types of rough terrain, assuming that is what you want. Engine horsepower also influences variables like size, weight, drivetrains, and even fuel types. Does the engine need to be internal combustion? Will it be electric? Turbine? Might it even be a hybrid that combines several types? I think I've made my point.

Protection

The type of armour protection on a tank can unbalance the previous two parameters without even meaning to. Will it be aluminum? Steel? That will make it heavier, thereby requiring more horsepower. Will it be composite (armour made up of a secret combination of steel and ceramic)? That will make it more expensive and so maybe a few dollars will need to be shaved off some other parts of the design. Will it be spaced (armour plates with air gaps between them)? That will make it more complicated and so may impact the overall design and weapons placements. Will it be reactive (armour that is explosive to counteract the energy of the incoming projectile)? This may also affect the placement of some of the weaponry, hatches, and so on. Will it be a mix of all three? And we haven't even touched upon where the protection will be thickest and where we might want to cut back a bit (traditionally, the top).

Phew, do we need to start over with the design?

CHARACTERISTICS

Note: When considering the characteristics below, realize that the list is a personal one and not from any particular army's doctrine.

All tanks share the same characteristics, and quite apart from tactics, the science and art of tank employment consists of combining and recombining these highly inter-related characteristics to best effect. Depending on which country's military manual you choose, the fundamental characteristics may differ, so I will discuss the whole array generically. Note that there is an overlap between several of the characteristics and design parameters. Why this is so should quickly become apparent. Generally, the characteristics are:

1. Firepower
2. Mobility
3. Armoured Protection;
4. Flexibility;
5. Shock Action; and
6. Inability to Hold Ground.

MBT Firing Positions

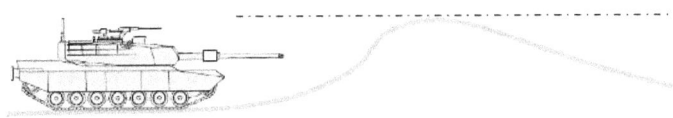

Turret Down (Tank invisible to direct line of sight)

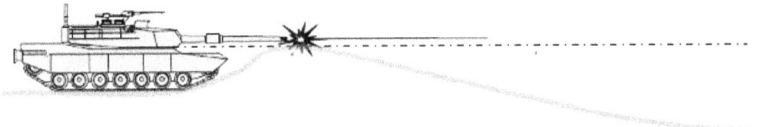

Hull Down (Hull invisible to direct line of sight)

Tracks Up (Tank visible to direct line of sight)

Firepower

Firepower is both a design parameter and an employment characteristic. Nothing characterizes tanks like their extraordinary direct firepower. Unless you have visited a tank range during live firing, it's difficult to fully appreciate the immense power of a tank's main gun, irrespective of caliber. This firepower can be brought to bear quickly and accurately in a wide range of battle scenarios. To give the uninitiated a flavour of what I mean, imagine being able to put a tungsten-carbide bullet that weighs almost five kilos, travelling at twice the speed of sound, through a large flat screen TV two kilometers away. Further, consider that the tank crew can do this while moving and sustain it at three rounds/minute for as long as there is ammunition in the vehicle.

Mobility

Like firepower, mobility is both a design parameter and an employment characteristic. Tanks are highly mobile, both on hard surfaces like roads as well as cross country. This is important not only for the individual tank, but just as important for the commander's ability to quickly shift these forces from one axis to another, from one enemy target to another. This characteristic is also related to flexibility, but only as seen from a higher commander's battlespace perspective. Naturally, this characteristic also brings limitations in that tanks cannot swim and can quickly become mired in mud and soft ground (consider the German problems during their attack on the USSR in World War II).

Armoured Protection

Again, although we have already looked at this characteristic, we need to revisit it because we are now considering it from an employment perspective rather than a design perspective (as we did already for firepower and mobility). The modern battlespace can be an extremely dangerous environment and although practically all soldiers now use personal body armour, nothing in the battlespace — I will say that again — *nothing in the battlespace* is protected to the extent that a tank is protected. What this means is that the tank can move into areas that other forces cannot, and thereby extend their protection to adjacent forces. They can act as shields for infantry and soft-skinned vehicles, provide protection during the clearing of obstacles, and even offer flank security simply by their physical presence.

Flexibility

This principle of war is also a characteristic of the tank. Because they can cover so many types of terrain, have a great deal of firepower using multiple weapons systems, are highly protected, and also have a variety of redundant communications systems, the commander can employ tanks in a wide variety of diverse tasks and roles, quite apart from simply engaging enemy in direct fire contests. And these diverse tasks can be accepted — and modified — quickly.

Shock Action

Napoleon mastered the employment of massed cavalry charges for shock action, or as he termed it, *masse de rupture*, which he employed to shatter enemy lines, as well as exploit success. What was true of heavy cavalry then, remains true of tank formations today. Of all the characteristics that tanks have, this one is arguably the least well understood. That said, in the hands of an aggressive and capable commander, the shock action of a large formation of tanks striking your position can be overwhelming. Having sat in a trench during a full-blooded assault by a British battle group based on a 59 MBT regiment as it rolled over our position, I can assure you that it is an event not soon forgotten.

Inability to Hold Ground

With advantages come disadvantages, and this characteristic is a loud warning to all armour commanders. However technologically advanced, powerful, fast, lethal, and protected, tanks may be, they are in the end tiny mobile fortresses and therefore cannot hold ground. Only dismounted troops can do that. Having said that, some militaries are doctrinally not particularly concerned with digging in and holding onto a piece of turf, and so don't consider this characteristic to be a meaningful drawback.

ROLES

Here we enter a grey zone because different military organizations view the proper employment of tanks differently. Rather than discuss this by specific military, let's look at the whole range of the things that tanks are expected to be able to do. Here are a few of the most obvious:

1. Engage the enemy directly;
2. Provide direct fire support to infantry;
3. Control key positions;
4. Protect vulnerable members of the combined arms team; and
5. Conduct recce and flanking actions.

VULNERABILITIES

In spite of having literally tons of active or inactive protective armour, tanks are by no means completely invulnerable, especially if they are employed incorrectly. (A great example of this fact is the demonstration of incompetent Russian tactics in the T90 video cited

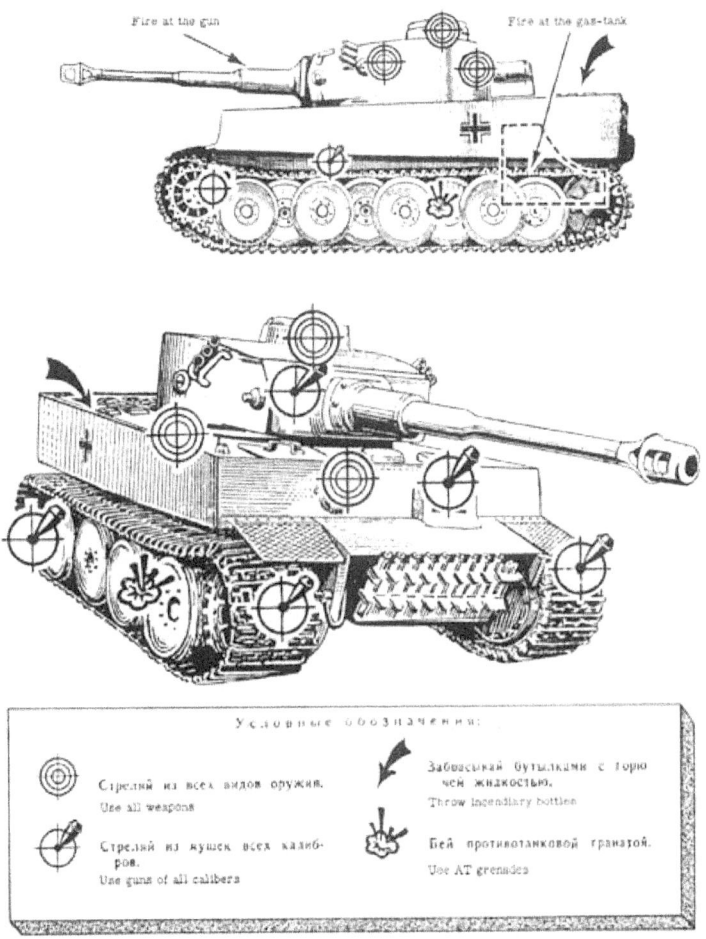

ABOVE: *Translated Soviet Army document, 1943.*

PART II: THE ART AND SCIENCE OF TANK EMPLOYMENT | 35

below in Part III.) Like all weapons systems, tanks have vulnerabilities. Below are the four greatest ones, and how tank crews and commanders work to minimize them.

1. Tanks cannot effectively defend themselves against dismounted forces in close combat. As a result, tanks endeavour to work hand in glove with infantry forces, who can provide safety and protection from dismounted enemy troops. When close support infantry is not readily at hand, there are drills and procedures to offer help. Sometimes, the ultimate solution is to avoid terrain (at least temporarily) that is too risky for tanks to venture into alone or unsupported.

2. Tanks can be highly vulnerable to anti-armour weapons. The ways to reduce the threat are as numerous as there are types of anti-armour weapons and range from adding special protection to the outside of the tank to training crews on immediate action drills on how to evade a guided missile once it has been fired at them.

3. Tanks are vulnerable to land mines. Properly emplaced minefields can stop any tank movement in its tracks if the crews are caught unaware. Again, tank troops have a collection of drills and procedures they can follow that range from engaging mine plows to clear the field, to using explosive devices to detonate the mines, to having supporting troops like combat engineers clear the routes as part of their mobility and anti-mobility battle tasks.

4. Tanks are always at high risk from top attack, whether from artillery, aircraft, or drones. This risk has grown dramatically with the increased employment of drones, but in essence has changed little from earlier days. Protective coverings are

now common and range from highly technical explosive armour to ersatz crude coverings made from chicken wire (drone cages). The most basic of all techniques is ensuring that the tank force employs air sentries, and where possible, air defence weapons.

Thus, it becomes apparent that the never-ending push and pull of measures and countermeasures continues, and every new weapon, and every new tactic, quickly spawns a method or a device to counteract its effectiveness. No vulnerabilities can be completely removed, but there are always effective ways to reduce them. Individually, crews have a collection of methods, as we have seen. Collectively, the answer is found in combined arms theory, already discussed above, which articulates the needs and the ways to build on strength and also cover weakness.

Armed with the design parameters, characteristics, and roles of tanks, let's now investigate the three subcomponents of the Armour branch and how tanks form the backbone of that branch.

ARMOURED FORCES

In Part I, I explained that "armour" is a generic term, encompassing a great deal of mechanized warfare and a word that has the potential to lead to confusion. First, there is "Armour" which is the name of the branch (like Infantry and Artillery), but which most often refers to MBTs. Then there is Armoured Recce, and Armoured Cav. Then there's "armoured artillery" (a.k.a. self-propelled artillery), "armoured infantry" (a.k.a. mechanized infantry), and finally "armoured engineers", which should now be self-explanatory. Here, we'll focus on those forces belonging to the Armour Branch as shown in the organization chart below.

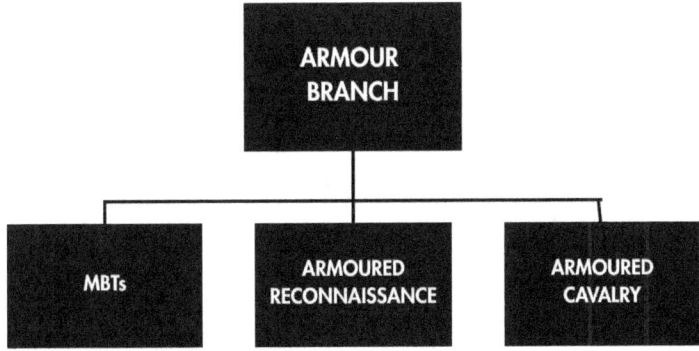

MAIN BATTLE TANKS (MBT)

Before proceeding, allow me to explain briefly why I now use the term "MBT". At its heart it is simply this: all MBTs are tanks, but not all tanks are MBTs. A tank is an armoured fighting vehicle (AFV), and as will be discussed below under the rubrics of Armoured Recce and Armoured Cav, it can be employed in a broad variety of different roles. But only when it's used in a certain way is a tank actually an MBT — a *Main Battle* Tank. Yet again we return to drawing a distinction between the equipment itself and how it's employed. If you're beginning to sense that this is not so simple, that's good. Very little about modern armoured warfare is.

The distinction I have insisted upon was first drawn during the Cold War and the first tank to be designated specifically as an MBT was the British Army's Chieftain, a sixty-ton behemoth that sported a devastatingly accurate Royal Ordnance 120 mm main gun. The Chieftain was so heavily protected there was little if anything that could penetrate its frontal armoured protection. This AFV was literally designed to roll into a battlespace and absorb hits while it destroyed oncoming Soviet forces. The Chieftain led the way in the 1960s, and other armies followed suit, moving toward the concept of having mostly MBTs in their fighting arsenals with only a few lighter AFVs designated for specialist functions.

MBTs, as opposed to other AFVs, are narrowly designed to provide fully protected direct fire and movement. Other AFVs may have some of its characteristics, but no other weapon system in the modern battlespace combines all of its functions in a single platform.

MBTs are designed to destroy targets through hypervelocity, highly accurate, rapid, direct fire. Their targets can be AFVs, including other MBTs, stationary defensive fortifications, soft targets like artillery vehicles, supply units, headquarters, infantry and even aircraft. Equipped with a large-caliber gun as its main armament, machine guns, and highly advanced computer-controlled fire control systems, MBTs are as accurate on the move as they are when stationary.

Last, but not least, what makes a tank an MBT is the crew and their mind-set. They know that their job is to fight, and they aggressively go forth looking for that fight. Speed and violence are their calling cards.

ARMOURED RECCE

If you can command tanks, you can learn to command armoured recce. If you can learn to command armoured recce, you can learn to command anything.

Captain H.R Wyant
Lord Strathcona's Horse (RC), 1976

Armoured Recce forces are closely-held resources that senior commanders guard jealously. This situation stems from the fact that these are highly trained troops with special skills. They act as the commanders' eyes and ears and are rarely if ever subordinated or "loaned" to junior commanders. Whereas MBT forces are always looking for a brawl, Armoured Recce may be looking for the enemy but almost never for a direct engagement with that enemy.

Unlike MBTs, Armoured Recce does not go where it's shoved, because it isn't looking for a fight. It goes where it needs to go, often out of contact with higher headquarters and on occasion, even behind enemy lines. Armoured Recce forces are not "pushed" towards an enemy; they "pull" friendly forces behind them to best find gaps and then exploit those gaps.

Armoured Recce is not based on any particular vehicle type. My first

SAMPLE ARMOURED RECCE TROOP

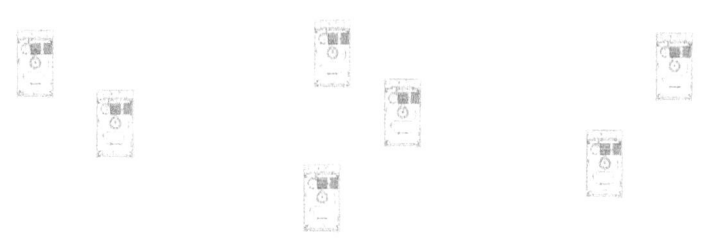

Note: An armoured recce troop can have any number of vehicles broken into two-car patrols.

commands as an Armoured Recce commander were a troop of four lightly armoured Lynx tracked vehicles and thereafter seven Korean War-vintage unprotected jeeps. The change of vehicles did not change my mission or my tactics, nor have an impact on my employment. I was the CO's eyes and ears.

The key factor was not the vehicle platform; it was what was between all of my crew commanders' ears. It was how they *thought*. Like my comment on the basis of Armour, the basis of Armoured Recce is mind-set. Recce commanders are sly, calculating, and wary. They want to avoid fighting for information if they can. They would rather not have the enemy know that they are in the area — especially if they are sitting in vulnerable vehicles and are not looking for trouble, because without armoured protection or heavy weapons, there is no way for them to fight themselves out of a bind.

As the quote above from my father-in-law, who in World War II and the Korean War was both an MBT and an Armoured Recce commander implies, it takes a special kind of soldier to be effective as an Armoured Recce soldier.

Every commander puts out recce forces to be the eyes and ears of the formation so that he may be apprised of what is going on in the battlespace and maintain situational awareness. It takes many years of training and practice to become proficient at all types of Armoured Recce, and such troops should always be employed with great care for once lost, they are not easily or quickly replaced.

From a Canadian perspective, most of what Armoured Recce does is covered below under Armoured Cav, but the key to understanding its effective use is simple: it's a scarce resource with hard-won skill sets.

Last, to put a lid on the idea that Armoured Recce is not vehicle type based (and to lead us into the next topic of Armoured Cav), my personal experience in changing vehicles from tracks to wheels can be extended to what friends of mine experienced in the *Bundeswehr*. At the height of the Cold War, German Leopard I tanks were used *both* as Armoured Recce and as MBTs, depending on the needs of the commander.

ARMOURED CAVALRY

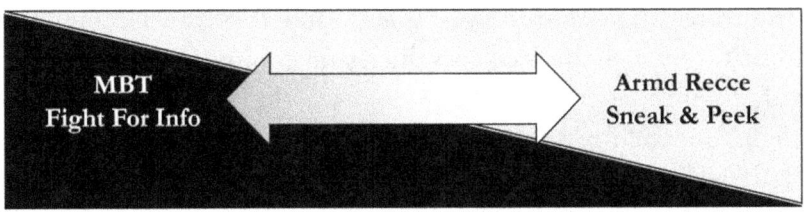

Fundamentally, Armoured Cav units are created by a melding of MBTs and Armoured Recce comprising two distinct types of AFVs, one heavy, the other light. As a result, it can be confusing to the uninitiated. The diagram above can act as a useful model to help us understand how MBTs and Armoured Recce act collectively to create Armoured Cav. The two wedges represent how Armoured Cav is employed, from fighting to sneaking about the battlespace. On the far left tanks are fighting as MBTs, using shock action and firepower. At the far right, the unit is fully in a recce role, using stealth and cunning. The key is in appreciating that the roles and tasks can be in constant flux, changing on a moment to moment basis. Recall the definitions earlier. The key difference between Armoured Cav and Armoured Recce is not equipment; it is *mindset*. Further, remember that we must not confuse the weapon with its employment. As you might imagine, such a unit requires soldiers and commanders at all levels with a special outlook. They must understand fully armour in all of its iterations. No mean feat.

Let's go deeper to investigate how individual MBTs and AFVs work together when used as Armoured Cav. Whenever I talk about tanks, I am adamant that tanks do not work effectively in small numbers. Annex A goes into this matter in some depth. Now I am going to contradict myself ... sort of. In an MBT troop, there are three or four tanks. That is simple enough. In an Armoured Recce troop there is a collection of AFVs, and they can be anything from rovers to light tracked vehicles up to and including tanks. For instance, some armies use doctrine that says that they will "fight" for their tactical information and to do so they use tanks. (I already mentioned the *Bundeswehr*.) Here is where many lose their way.

If we see four tanks sitting together, is it an MBT troop? Is it and Armoured Recce troop? Or is it an Armoured Cav troop?

The answer is that it depends, and you cannot determine the answer by simply looking at them.

If a man is standing in an open space holding a sharp knife in his hand, what is he? Maybe he is a chef. Maybe he is a butcher. Maybe he is a Special Forces (SF) soldier. Without knowing more than simply what tool he wields, it's impossible to know *what* he is. Context is key. Further, without knowing what that individual's skillset is, you cannot have the whole picture, so do not focus on the equipment. Appreciate the need to consider the equipment, the training *and* the intent.

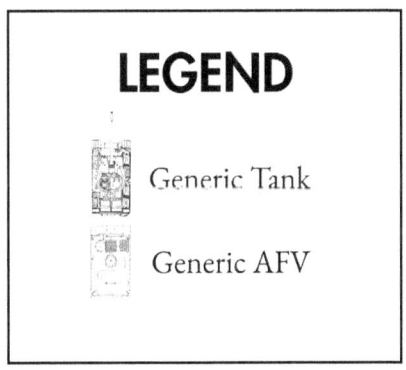

Back to the tanks. Beyond the obvious fact that these tanks we observe are fearsome combat weapons, the answer to the question above is not so simple. This is because we need to know who the

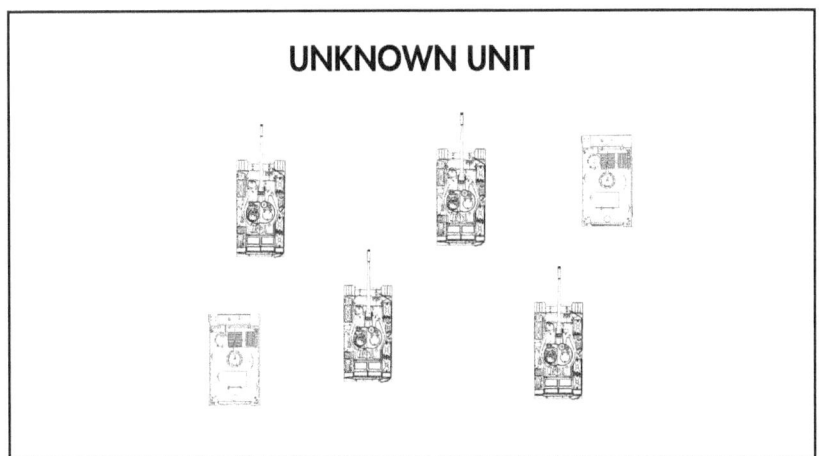

commanders are and what their mindsets are. If the commanders are trained as part of a tank battalion, then they likely comprise an MBT troop. Likewise, for Recce. But what if they are trained to do both, depending on their mission? Then they are Armoured Cav and based on what the commander wants, they can be chameleons and change back and forth from MBT to Recce as required. Some specifics will help clarify.

In the same way that you couldn't determine what the man holding the knife was just from looking at him, you cannot tell what a group is just from looking at it. What might this unknown unit above be?

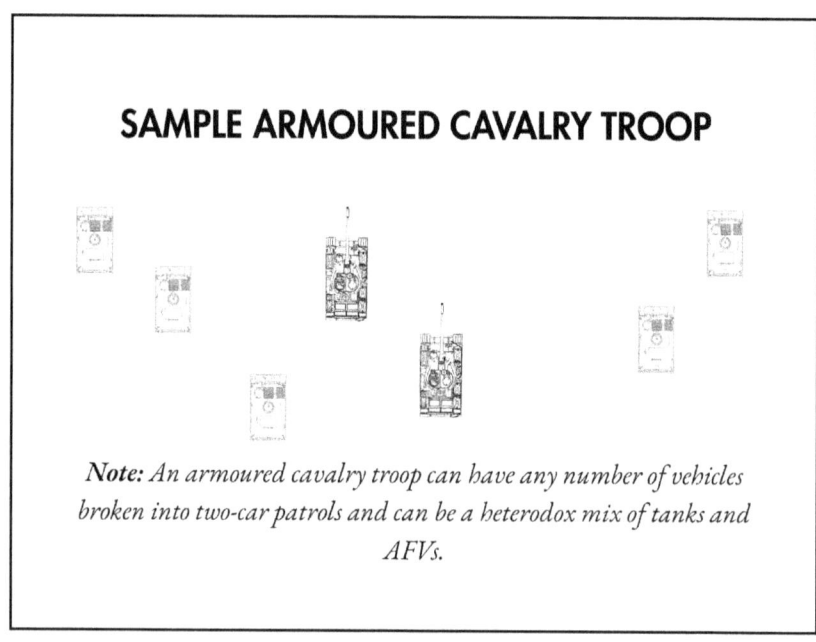

SAMPLE ARMOURED CAVALRY TROOP

Note: An armoured cavalry troop can have any number of vehicles broken into two-car patrols and can be a heterodox mix of tanks and AFVs.

The possibilities are legion. It could be a tank troop with a couple of infantry sections (or squads) or even a combat recce patrol. But since we are investigating Armoured Cav, let's consider that it might be a troop of Armoured Cav, since Cav troops are configured to meet their missions.

Above is another variant that is just as viable as an Armoured Cav troop. As I said, the variations are unlimited.

Why bother mixing tanks and lighter vehicles? The answer is that they each overcome a weakness in the other, just like combined arms teams. Tanks can fight but have difficulty with "sneak and peek". The opposite is true of "light" Armoured Recce vehicles. What the mix gives you is the flexibility to hold the tanks back while you gain battlespace intelligence or add them early to do "recce by fire" whereby you go out looking for a reaction so that you can try to have the enemy tip their hand regarding their disposition and intent.

EMPLOYMENT OF TANKS

As with everything, success is based on choosing the appropriate tool and then employing it well. Recall the admonition from one of my instructors that "*misuse* is *abuse.*" Otherwise stated, not using a piece of equipment properly is worse than not using it at all. Successful tank tactics depend on doctrine matching circumstances. In my view, at the intellectual level tank doctrine is basically bifurcated, that is to say it breaks itself into two schools. The Germanic armies look at it one way, and the Anglo-Saxon armies look at it in another. All other armies fall more or less into one of these two camps. Tanks are used to either:

1. Embrace battlespace chaos and fight the manoeuvre battle (Germanic); or
2. Reinforce static battle positions held by infantry (Anglo-Saxon).

These two schools are generic and leave plenty of room for variations, but one variation that is thorny is the tactic of employing single tanks on their own. There is a time and place for such tactics, but they are highly specific, and their employment is fraught with controversy. (the Russian T90 example later in the book). For Afghanistan veterans, this tactic was common, but that was a unique operating environment. I purposely don't want to go down that road here because from my personal perspective, using individual tanks in conventional war is an *advanced* warfighting technique that should only be used with highly experienced troops and commanders, and it's an issue that falls outside the limited purview of this book.

Both schools of employment offer valid options, and no single solution will fit every situation. But before a commander begins her analysis, and after she has asked herself what exactly "decisive action" means, she must consider whether the situation calls for the tanks to force chaos or whether employing tanks will have the aim of helping the infantry in whatever they are doing. This decision is fundamental and will dictate how not only the tanks are employed, but also all the other AFVs in the combined arms team.

As an armour officer, I spent my career routinely frustrated by commanders (of all arms) who misemployed me and my forces. In the RCAC, we loved to complain about this misuse and abuse, but no one, not even generals who were armour officers, ever corrected this problem. To be fair to my brother combat arms officers (there were almost no women in the combat arms then), this misuse was firmly rooted in our doctrine and so it was difficult to fault them. But this doctrine was clearly an entrenchment of outdated practices we had used during the invasion and liberation of Europe in 1944-45. Like my earlier anecdote about General Rad, the battlespace had changed but our doctrine never did — not even when armour officers rose to become the Army Commander.

The two schools of tank employment, with their different mindsets, are quite distinct, but not mutually exclusive. The Germanic school is focused on rapid movement and manoeuvre, both in offence and defence, whether it's with mechanized infantry or armoured forces, and sees the shock action of the MBT as a characteristic to be exploited whenever possible. It doesn't see the tank as a weapon that is primarily in the battlespace to aid and support the infantry. Most important, there is little or no attempt to bring order to something that is understood as fundamentally chaotic, that is to say, combat.

The second, Anglo-Saxon school, certainly recognizes the characteristics and capabilities of armour in general, and the MBT in particular, but its fundamental understanding of warfare stems from the desire for a set-piece battle. Chaos is to be avoided, not exploited. The desire to order the battlespace underlies this philosophy, and commanders work to control the chaos in any way possible.

MBT EMPLOYMENT

In order to be the combat arm of decision, armour commanders must be bold. The definition of armour is usually based on vehicle type, but not always. One thing remains constant: the concept of armoured warfare is *always* based on mindset. Armour commanders need to be aggressive, whether they are leading MBT forces, Recce or Cav. Later, in Part III, we'll see examples of how mindset is more important than equipment, but for the time being, it should be clear that if armour forces are not fought with aggression and boldness, they are being less than optimally employed. Here is the best way to think about the MBT: It goes where it is pushed, so push it! The whole point of having a weapon based on shock action is to shock the enemy with it.

During my time as an armour commander, as well as my time as an instructor, I *always* made a great fuss about the splitting of MBT squadrons. It became a running joke amongst my subordinates, and my students. The reason I was so single-minded about this issue was plain and simple: splitting squadrons greatly reduces combat power by relegating the tank commanders, who are experts in shock, firepower, and manoeuvrer to merely controlling mobile gun platforms, unable to fully exploit the full range of the tanks' capabilities.

The reason for this reduction requires an explanation, and boils down to two key reasons, both of which affect combat power:

1. Command; and
2. Logistics.

Each of these two issues is discussed later in much greater detail. Command is discussed in Annex A and Logistics in Annex B, but for now, let's move on to how best to *kill* tanks.

ARMOUR VS ANTI-ARMOUR

I've already said that MBTs should not be the primary weapon system to kill other MBTs. Yes, they may be the *best* weapon to do that, but if you use them that way as their *primary* role, you greatly lessen the opportunities to build combat power. Let's look at why.

When the first tanks fought on the Somme in 1916, there was practically nothing that could stop them. That quickly changed and by the time tanks became common in the battlespace two decades later, several weapons had been designed *specifically* to kill tanks. There is now a wide spectrum of weaponry that is optimized to knock out MBTs. The primary method is by Anti-Tank Guided Missile (ATGM) and disregarding those launched from the air, these weapons systems primarily belong to the infantry, which can choose from well over one hundred different missiles, from shoulder-launched, to tripod-launched, to vehicle-launched.

Inexperienced tank commanders crave open vistas to maximize their ability to hit targets quickly and accurately at long ranges. But any tank commanders who have been in the crosshairs of a TOW or

Eryx missile gunner know better. The inexpert commander does not appreciate that good tank country is also good anti-tank country. That is not to say that tanks need to avoid open country with long ranges, but all commanders need to understand the trade-offs. An MBT can easily put three tungsten-carbide rounds into an object one-meter square at over three kilometers in under a minute. Highly trained tank crews can do this even faster — and while moving! But the growing family of ATGMs is nearly as accurate, and in some cases, can exceed the range of the tank gun. That said, their disadvantages are two-fold: these missiles are rocket-propelled, which fly much slower than the hypersonic tank rounds; and the gunners are not as well-protected by armour as are the tank crews.

The problem with the debate on who would win the MBT vs ATGM fight is that it <u>misses the point</u>. Each weapon system has a purpose to which it's best suited. The key to tactical success is in understanding the strengths and weaknesses of each of the weapon systems at your disposal and then optimally combining the diverse systems to build combat power. The whole construct of combined arms theory rests upon this foundation.

What makes combined arms theory work is the idea that the strength of one arm more than compensates for the weakness of another and as you combine multiple combat arms to form a team, you radically diminish these weaknesses and dramatically increase these strengths. You are enabling synergy. The conclusion of this debate may not be obvious: learn to employ your weapons creatively and to best effect. Yes, tanks can quickly kill other tanks, but if that's what they are doing, their ability to destroy your enemy's softer — and possibly more important targets — is greatly diminished. Thus, you have *reduced* your combat power.

This issue is discussed using a detailed scenario in Annex C below.

INTERIM CONCLUSIONS

We have covered a great deal in this second part of the book, so it is worth the effort to quickly summarize and solidify what we have investigated, and I hope, learned.

I have stated that the acquisition of the necessary knowledge and expertise to effectively both understand and practise armoured warfare begins as a science and grows into an art form as one progresses in skill and comprehension. In order to investigate this claim, I began this section with tank design and characteristics. We saw that the three fundamental design parameters of Firepower, Mobility, and Protection were universal in all tank design and that creating an equilibrium among them was no small task. In fact, it was tremendously challenging and was strongly influenced by the warfighting culture of the country in which the tank was being designed.

We then moved to the characteristics inherent in all tanks (irrespective of how they were used) and the astute reader should have begun to see that there were proper and improper ways to apply these various characteristics. We had begun our journey away from the *science* of armoured warfare and toward the *art* of armoured warfare.

That then allowed us to proceed to the three major divisions within what is broadly known as the Armour Branch, namely, MBT, Armoured Recce and Armoured Cav. This is where the paradoxes of armoured warfare — especially for the uninitiated — seemed to grow, page by page. The same vehicle, depending on its employment at the hands of a skilled soldier or commander, could fulfil an incredible range of tasks and functions, sometimes simultaneously.

It was with this dissection of the tripartite Armour Branch that it should have become increasingly obvious that whatever killing power or protection the tank inherently had, the characteristic that made it so uniquely valued as a member of the combined arms team was its unmatched flexibility. No other weapon system in modern warfare can perform such a wide variety of tasks and functions by itself, and no other weapon system can bring so much value to a sister combat arm, when employed correctly.

We did not skip over the tank's vulnerabilities for like all weapon systems, it could fall prey to adversarial weapons, but it was clear that much of the vulnerability inherent in tank employment lay in its misemployment. Whatever the claims of new weapons making the mechanized goliaths of the battlefield no longer viable, when employed in the hands of experienced and skillful commanders, tank forces were not only deadlier than ever, they were quite literally irreplaceable.

PART III: REAL WORLD BATTLE

INTRODUCTION

We'll now briefly examine four examples of tank employment to demonstrate what I've been arguing. The point of the examples is not to review the battles in detail but rather to demonstrate how the three key points I have mentioned are borne out by real-life examples.

Keep these three key arguments in mind while looking at the examples:

1. The ultimate determinant of success is the proper/improper employment of armoured forces generally and MBTs in particular.
2. Technology is an enabler not a decider and neither is numerical or firepower superiority.
3. The human commander with the correct mentality and skill set is more important than vehicle type. The proper employment of an armoured force is not based on vehicle type; it's *always* based on mind-set.

EXAMPLE I: FRANCE MAY 1940

In 1940, the German Wehrmacht won an extraordinary battle with France and her allies in six short weeks. Often held up as an example of *Blitzkrieg*,[2] it was more accurately the demonstration *par excellence* of combined arms battle in general and the employment of tanks in particular.

The idea of rapid warfare was not new for the Germans, having experimented with this idea since the Wars of German Unification in the mid 19th century. The mechanization of the modern army along with the German Army's strong adherence to Combined Arms Theory allowed it to stun the Allies with their relentless maneuvering and application of combat power.

Before hostilities began, the French and their allies had all the advantages but lost anyway. Between them the Allies had almost 4,000 tanks. The Germans had approximately 2,500. Force size was approximately equal with almost 3.3 million soldiers on each side. French tanks were technically superior in almost every respect and yet they lost almost 1,800 of them. Although the British tanks were

---

2. *Blitzkrieg or "lightning war" was not a doctrine or even a term used by the German Army. It was the <u>outcome</u> of many decades of tactical thinking about Bewegungskreig or "war of (rapid) movement." The introduction of tanks finally brought this German thinking to its point of fruition.*

on par with the Germans, they too, suffered heavy losses with almost 700 destroyed. German tank losses in May and June of 1940 were approximately 800 of all types. One is left to wonder why.

The answer lies in a combination of doctrine and leadership philosophy. German forces were integrated combined arms teams and leaders at all levels were imbued with the belief that aggression was how tanks were to be used and that infantry was to support this aggression. In broad terms, the Allies did neither. There were indeed commanders on the Allied side who wanted to fight tanks as the Germans did, namely a young tank colonel by the name of Charles de Gaulle, but his ideas ran counter to French doctrine. French tanks were frequently emplaced in static positions, relying on their heavy armor and powerful guns. By comparison German panzers, lighter and less powerfully gunned, emphasized mobility, thereby outflanking and isolating defenders.

The German combined arms formations, most famously the *Panzer Group Kleist* (General Paul Ludwig von Kleist), *XIX Panzer Korps* (General Heinz Guderian), the *7. Panzerdivision* (General Erwin Rommel), and the *XLI Panzer Korps* (General Georg-Hans Reinhardt) attacked on narrow frontages with tanks, broke through the French defences and then raced westward for the English Channel. The pace of the advance was terrifying with often unguarded flanks in excess of 200 kilometers! At times these commanders were so far away from their superior headquarters that their commanders — although they were trying — could not slow them down.

Within weeks the French Army collapsed with most of it not having fought anything more than skirmishes. The British Expeditionary Force (BEF), refusing to surrender, retreated to Dunkirk and was rescued by one of the most valiant operations in the history of warfare — but without its equipment.

The Wehrmacht achieved both an astounding and a decisive victory due to better employment of forces and doctrine and NOT because of any superiority in their soldiers or their equipment.

Two key battles during the invasion prove the point. At the village of Hannut, Belgium, one of the largest tank engagements up to that point saw French S35 tanks best German panzers but German commanders outmanoeuvred the defenders and went around them, making their positions irrelevant. At Arras, a BEF counter offensive caught the Germans off-guard and the British Matilda tanks could not be destroyed by anti-tank guns. The Germans beat the exhausted British by constant counterattacks, and by innovating. They used their 88 mm anti-aircraft guns in an anti-tank role.

EXAMPLE II: YOM KIPPUR WAR 1973

The fourth of the Arab-Israeli wars began on 6 October 1973, the holiest day of the Jewish calendar, Yom Kippur, when in a strategic surprise attack Syria and Egypt invaded Israel simultaneously on two fronts, Syria from the northeast and Egypt from the southwest across the Suez Canal. The war lasted only twenty days and came within a hair of ending the existence of the state of Israel, with Israeli tank crews widely credited as being the saviours of the nation. [3]

The element of surprise was almost complete. Egyptian forces crossed the canal with far fewer casualties than expected while Syrian forces quickly reached the strategic Golan Heights, northwest of Lake Tiberias, and critical to the strategic safety of Israel. It was here, in the Valley of Tears (*Emek Ha-Bacha*), that Israel's future lay, and so it's to this battle that we now turn.

Defending the Golan was one reinforced IDF armoured brigade of about 100 refitted British Centurian tanks (The IDF dubbed this MBT the Sho't Kal). On the Syrian side stood three infantry divisions

---

[3] *General Rafael Eitan, Chief of the Israeli General Staff speaking to IDF armoured corps soldiers: "If we had not stopped the Syrians on the Golan Heights, then the State of Israel would have been destroyed…This division saved Israel from defeat, from catastrophe…I want to stress and make it clear to you; you saved the people of Israel. First and foremost, you!"*

with a total of approximately 300 tanks, a combination of the Soviet T55 and newer T62 (with night-fighting optics). Importantly, behind the three infantry divisions sat two Syrian armoured divisions, each with 250 tanks, as well as two independent Syrian tank brigades, each with 120 tanks as well as a Moroccan brigade. The Syrian objective was to take the Heights in order to control all of the Golan and thereby have a direct axis of advance in to the heart of Israel. During the first three days of battle, the Israeli 7th Tank Brigade was almost destroyed, but managed to hold on, just barely. By all appearances the odds were overwhelmingly on the Syrian side, both in numbers and in technology with newer tanks that could fight at night. That said, the Syrians did not exploit their early successes, and the IDF hung on.

By the morning of the fourth day there was one lone battalion remaining on the Israeli side to deny the Heights. It was the 77th Armoured Battalion (known as Oz 77) commanded by 29-yr-old Lieutenant colonel Avigdor Kahalani.[4] The Syrians launched a massive attack with hundreds of tanks moving up out of the valley. Kalahani's 40 tanks were the final bulwark against more than 500 Syrian tanks. His men had been fighting non-stop for more than two days, and he gave orders to move but discovered that his exhausted men refused to fight, so he pushed off to the high ground alone, determined to die fighting. Upon cresting the high ground, he confronted three T62s at under 100 meters. He destroyed the first, then the second one closed to 50 meters before he knocked it out. Then his guns jammed. Suddenly the third tank exploded, having been struck by a tank that followed him to the top. His action was the turning point in a battle that was itself a turning point in the war. The remainder of his subordinates rushed to join him and for the remainder of the day

---

[4] I had the honour of speaking with General Kahalani when he was a guest on a video battlefield study of the Yom Kippur War. He described the last day of battle in intimate detail and was quite modest when asked about winning Isreal's Medal of Valor, Israel's equivalent of the Commonwealth Victoria Cross.

the exhausted battalion fought off waves of Syrian tank attacks. That evening the Syrians, having lost over 250 tanks and twice that many armoured infantry vehicles, quit the field.

The war proved costly. All three belligerents suffered high casualties both in terms of personnel as well as military materiel. As with the Germans in France, the Israelis, through violent and bold action overcame numeric and technological inferiority to win, not only in the Golan but also retaking the Sinai Peninsula from the Egyptians, again with similar tank tactics.

EXAMPLE III: GULF WAR I 1991

During Gulf War I the US deployed 1,500 Abrams M1A2 MBTs against Iraq's over 4,000 Soviet-made tanks of various types. I was a staff officer in Canada's European HQ and can attest that anxiety levels were high among NATO allies. The Iraqis had one of the largest MBT forces in the world, and many pundits were reminding everyone that the Iraqis not only had a massive tank army, but they were battle-hardened after having fought an eight-year war with Iran, which had ended only three years earlier. On top of it all, the Iraqis had the advantage of being on the defensive and fully dug in.

I am not prescient, nor am I a genius — or even close. After one high-level security briefing before the war began, I quietly predicted to several people in the room that the war would not be a long, drawn out, bloody affair. I predicted that the coalition would defeat the Iraqis in a week. My colleagues just smirked. I based my prediction on years of study and what I was taught during two rigorous courses (six months at the Canadian Army Command and Staff College and twenty-four months at the German Armed Forces Command and General Staff College). I simply did not see anything in what I had read, or heard, (including classified material) that suggested the Iraqis understood how to employ armour — in any of its variants —

or that they had a grasp of combined arms theory. Oil money had bought thousands of Soviet tanks and AFVs, but it could not buy expertise (even if the Soviets had had any real expertise to offer!).

I was wrong; the war didn't last a week. It only lasted 100 hours. The outcome is now well known, and I won't go back over the incredible performance of the US Army's historied 2nd Armored Cavalry Regiment during the Battle of 73 Easting. But the numbers only tell part of the story. Let's begin there:

Based on open sources, in four days of combat the US Army lost:

- 31 x M1 MBTs (destroyed or disabled)
- 28 x Bradley IFVs (destroyed or disabled)
- 1 x M113 APC (destroyed)

Conversely, in four days of combat the Iraqi Army lost approximately:

- 3,300 x MBTs of various types (destroyed)
- 2,100 x APCs of various types (destroyed)

Artillery weapons losses and personnel casualties are even starker by comparison, if that is possible to imagine.

What can we glean from the numbers? Lots. These losses are truly staggering. Surely they were a result of far more than first-rate tanks and IFVs fighting second rate weapons, and they were. The story the numbers tell is about employment.

The Iraqis tied almost all of their tanks to static dug in positions. The whole point of using MBTs is that they can *manoeuvre* and although there was a limited amount of that attempted by the elite Republican Guard units, even that limited use was done badly. The Iraqis fought in isolated single arm formations whereas the Allies fought as integrated combined arms forces. Armoured Cavalry led with Armoured Recon, MBTs and combat engineers, opening paths for follow-on MBT/IFV combat teams of various sizes and compositions. Artillery was ever-present both to kill Iraqi artillery as well as — and more importantly — to support the manoeuvre of the combined arms attacking forces.

EXAMPLE IV: UKRAINE 2024

There is a terrific video available on the internet of a close-battle encounter between a Russian T90 M MBT (Their most advanced tank, sporting a 125 mm main gun) and a Ukrainian-crewed older version US Bradley IFV, which is not the most up-to-date model, sporting a 25 mm Bushmaster chain gun. The T90 was specifically designed to defeat other MBTs. This contest should have been a no-brainer: Tank sees the IFV, tank kills the IFV, tank moves to the next target. Clearly, once the MBT spotted the IFV, the tank should have obliterated the smaller, less well-protected and less well-armed vehicle.[5]

But that is *not* what happened.

The engagement begins with footage from a drone hovering over the ruins of a small town. It's January with snow covering the fields. The Ukrainians were fighting a mobile defence against Russian tanks that were attempting to take the town when a Bradley comes within mere meters of a T90. The MBT sees the Bradley and fires point blank but misses.

---

[5] *Here is the link to the video. It is presented by the British Army's BFBS radio system with commentary. https://www.youtube.com/watch?v=yrrso5JDR5I*

This is the second, and inevitably fatal, mistake. Why second? What was a T90 MBT doing all on its own? Anyway, the Russian crew was so close that it could have hit the Bradley with a rock! The IFV crew, instead of reversing, charges forward towards the tank. It engages with its chain gun and begins peppering the MBT's turret, while making a run for cover. The MBT returns fire twice more and misses *twice more.*

The Bradley now makes its escape but, like all good AFV crews, its movement was being covered by a second IFV, (see my comment above regarding the T90's first mistake) which now moves toward the MBT, firing as it approaches. These IFV crew commanders show both aggression and offensive spirit, whereas the MBT crew seems to be at a loss. It should have easily destroyed *both* IFVs.

The second IFV commander purposely targets the MBT turret because he knows that nothing he has on board can penetrate the T90's armour. And here we have the key to the Ukrainian victory. The IFV commander opts to use high explosive ammo, designed to kill soft-skinned targets. This ammo destroys the MBT's suite of high-tech optics and sensors. The MBT, with a direct line of sight to the "tracks up" Bradley, which is now only a couple of hundred meters away, does not fire back. The Bradley continues to fire and the damage to the MBT increases. Eventually the tank catches fire and the turret begins to spin out of control as the T90 crew attempts to run for its life.

Eventually, the Russians crash their MBT and bail out. A Ukrainian drone then finishes off the wounded tank. There is much to unpack in this short engagement beginning with the idiotic idea that an MBT can idly roam in the battlespace without accompanying forces, whether they are other MBT or infantry. A sole tank wandering about is akin to a lone elk that's been abandoned by the herd. The wolves will be on it in an instant, and no matter how powerful the elk may be, it's doomed.

THE FUTURE

What does the future hold for mechanized warfare in general and AFVs and MBTs in particular? The truth, of course, is that no one can predict the future, but what is certain is that a key component will be technology, since historically, technology has always been a key prime mover in weapons' development. Below is a brief comment on a few (but not all) technological trends that may have an impact on armoured warfare and tanks.

LIGHTWEIGHT ARMOUR

Like stealth, the dream of impenetrable armour is as old as Greek mythology and the armour made for Achilles. We have not yet reached that dream but in the last few decades the advances in armour protection, have been remarkable. With passive armour plating, it's no longer a question of how thick the steel is, but also a question of what kind of hybrid alloy was used to make it. Further, the introduction of explosive reactive armour (ERA), where an explosive layer designed to detonate *away* from the vehicle, has introduced heretofore unimagined protection and there doesn't seem to be an upper limit to this technology.

ENERGY WEAPONS AND ADVANCE MUNITIONS

One of the greatest leaps forward in MBT design was supposed to be the introduction of directed energy weapons (DEWs), which use concentrated bursts of energy (either electromagnetic or particle) to destroy targets, rather than relying on kinetic energy like conventional weapons. When I was a young troop leader in the 70s, the rail gun energy weapon was supposed to make the solid shot projectile obsolete. They have been built and tested and never put into production. The next breathless prediction is lasers. We'll see.

Simultaneously, advances in solid shot kinetic weapons, whether in metallurgy or the chemistry of propellants, continue to allow MBTs to "reach out and touch" opponents at ever-longer ranges and faster and faster speeds. Interesting to be sure, but most tank engagements occur at less than 1,000 meters and the current munitions already travel at twice the speed of sound. One is left to wonder why we need bigger and faster rounds ....

HYBRID ENGINES

If you are a fan of Formula 1 racing, you will know that almost every new automobile made today has F1 to thank for some of the astounding hybrid technology that allows smaller engines to produce astounding amounts of power and torque. This permits AFVs to have more capacity for both armour and bigger guns since it affects the three-way balance already discussed above. Many auto manufactures (Volvo and Mercedes) no longer put pure internal combustion engines in their vehicles. Hybrid and hybrid electric appear to be the future.

NETWORKED BATTLEFIELD

Arguably nothing has made such astounding advancements in AFVs as has communications and the associated digital revolution in how AFVs can share information, both among themselves as well as back to higher headquarters. All this technology works to give the fighting crews better situational awareness in the battlespace, which translates directly into the ability to build and apply combat power appropriate to the tactical situation.

BUT.

All of this data and information *still* relies on humans. Will Artificial Intelligence (AI) take human commanders out of the loop? I don't believe it will. Warfare remains a human endeavour — at least for the foreseeable future.

AI ASSISTED OR CONTROLLED

This is a large category, and I will not look at all of it, but generally speaking, they refer to *Autonomous Systems* that do their work either uncontrolled by humans or by a combination of AI and human guidance. Much of what is termed AI has actually been built into our systems for decades. Cars have various levels of cruise control and automatic braking (completely controlled by computer *without* human input) and similar technology is now being developed for weapons systems that automatically track and destroy incoming weaponry. Israel's Iron Dome air defence system, for instance, autonomously tracks, identifies and intercepts incoming rockets, missiles and aircraft. Similar, smaller systems are developed for weaponry at the tactical level for ground forces.

The same is true for targeting and what used to be reserved for long range aerial combat has for decades been trialed in armoured warfare. The French Army's Leclerc XLR MBT, which has for decades had auto-enemy target recognition software has recently upgraded its fire control computers with integrated AI enemy detection software — but there is still a commander and still a gunner.

These AI incremental enhancements have been with us for decades. I trained on Centurion MBT that used hand cranks to move the main gun and an optical graticule sight (like binoculars). By the time I commanded my Leopard MBT, the graticule was gone and had been replaced with a single laser dot. Put the dot on the target and squeeze the trigger.

I do not mean to be dismissive because I support all of these advancements. But the human factor remains, and it remains the *key* component. All of these enhancements are really part of the battlespace requirement that every commander needs: situational awareness and the high-speed data fusion that synthesizes optical inputs, thermal imagery, radar and more remain adjuncts to the commander, whether she is commanding a single tank or a battalion of them.

ABOVE: *Experimental 7.2 inch rocket launcher mounted on a Sherman chassis.*

DRONES VS TANKS

I have purposely left this topic to the end because, to quote Shakespeare in *Hamlet*, I believe that drones are "more light than heat, extinct in both, even in their promise, as it is a-making." To be blunt, I am profoundly skeptical that drones have made any kind of *fundamental* change in warfare. Allow me to explain.

Drone warfare is over a century old, with the first remotely controlled aerial drone having been accomplished by the Royal Flying Corps in March of 1917. There were sporadic advances made, either by radio or wire guidance over the next century — think about torpedoes, antitank guided missiles, and rockets — and ironically, the latest "innovation" is the use of optical fibre. Nonetheless, the point is that they are *not* new. That said, their use in Ukraine has prompted some wild predictions (mostly by uninformed pundits), some even foreseeing the end of the MBT's dominance in modern warfare. Ukraine has had remarkable success with small first-person view (FPV) drones striking tanks from the air, and it's easy to be mesmerized by videos of these drones. Let's begin by briefly looking at drones in the broader context of military theory, and combined arms theory.

There is no evidence that drones can accomplish policy aims in war.

In that respect, they are like submarines. They can deny parts of the battlespace but can't control it. (Ukraine has denied much of the Black Sea to the Russian fleet but doesn't control it.) Like submarines, drones work within already accepted military theory, meaning they're *not* revolutionary. They're evolutionary. From our perspective, they're another anti-tank weapon. The question, therefore, is really *how much* have they changed the way we employ tanks. Are drones actually a major threat to tanks?

Well, I've seen this movie before. Several times. Before even completing my basic armour training, most of my classmates over at the Infantry School were eager to tell me that AT-3 Sagger missiles had made tanks obsolete. They were wrong. I heard it again (but louder) when TOW under armour missiles were developed. Wrong again. Then it was all about anti-tank helicopters. Wrong again. Then it was all about artillery deliverable scatterable mines (FASCAM) … You can see where I'm going.

Don't misunderstand me. All of the above weapons systems — and many, many, more — are powerful additions to the all arms fight and in the right hands, can be absolutely deadly threats to tanks. No argument there. But that misses the point. There is nothing new here. Obviously the advancement of drone use has changed current warfare, but as I've already explained, warfare changes almost daily. Has it fundamentally changed how MBTs are employed? Short answer, NO.

New technology has always had this effect on tactics, doctrine, and even force structure. Earlier I mentioned that a commander's goal is always to build combat power. To do so the commander works within combined arms theory and practice. Have drones changed how we use combined arms in the battlespace? No, they have not. Drones are easily integrated into the combined arms team, but nothing that they bring to the battlespace replaces any other weapons system. For instance, they cannot replace the shock action or firepower of armour. They cannot hold ground like infantry. They cannot provide mobility or counter-mobility like combat engineers. They cannot provide massive suppression like artillery. Drones cannot protect, take, or retake terrain, control a portion of a battlespace by their very presence, clear hostile forces from an objective, or project combat power.

Further, drones cannot destroy enemy forces while simultaneously protecting one's own forces. This is a key aspect of tank/infantry cooperation that is easily overlooked when praising the value of drones. Drones may assist infantry in taking an objective but consider the wide variety of abilities required to keep what has been gained and it becomes clear that drones fall short. They cannot, for instance, survive an artillery barrage or even operate in all types of weather. The list goes on.

Ukraine's creative and profuse employment of drones has captured social media but has made almost no positive strategic difference. Unlike tanks, drones have not captured Russian territory or recaptured Ukrainian territory In fact, drone use on both sides has made what should be a mobile war into a static one, making it ever-more attritional and positional. We are watching a return to Flanders in 1916, with the expansion of trench lines and bunkers, and I remind you that it wasn't until the introduction of tanks to the battlefield that mobility was restored and ultimate victory achieved. Drones are indeed cheaper than tanks, but their use is denying resources to mobile forces like MBTs and IFVs — with their deadly accompanying firepower. Perhaps this denial is not intentional, but it is a consequence of drone use. Imagine what a massive increase in the number of Ukrainian MBTs would have done.

FPV drones are really just another version of aerial bombardment, a tactic that has never been proven successful in dislodging entrenched military forces if they are determined to hold ground. Such tactics merely force the defender to better protect themselves. Our bloody experiences in all modern ground wars should have taught us this, but it seems we may not have learned the lesson quite yet.

SUMMARY

Clearly, FPV drones have been game-changing in many ways. Armoured forces have to be more vigilant, but that was always true. Nonetheless, drones' inability to control key points makes them less useful than they may appear. Their usage is important, but their limitations and inability to operate protected in all weather and indefinitely sustained, make them valuable tools to be *added* to the arsenal and not *replacements* of anything already there — especially not the MBT or any other armoured forces. Flooding the battlespace with drones may stave off defeat, but victory only comes from the offence and as I have demonstrated, no weapon system in the modern battlespace offers the combat power of the MBT, both offensively and defensively, whether tactically, operationally or strategically.

Drones undoubtedly are a threat to tanks — especially as we have seen with Russian tank crews — when the crews are poorly trained or employed. But well trained and competently employed crews have no more to fear from drones than from any other anti-tank weapon, and there are hundreds. By comparison with what tanks can achieve, drones have demonstrated that they are effective single use weapons, which do little more than remove individual targets — albeit sometimes quite spectacularly — and this is where the argument against MBTs comes off the rails.

A single drone killing a single tank is not the harbinger of doom for the MBT. As I write *The New York Times* has made this very mistake in a beautifully illustrated article that completely misses the point: Putting up nets or cages or boxes to protect tanks from drones may *seem* like a radical change, but it is not. From 1917 on, soldiers have been finding immediate solutions to their tactical problems. In the 1940s Canadian tank crews added extra track pads to the front of their Shermans in the hopes of surviving a strike from a German 88. Drones have made an impact, but none of it is fundamental.

The Ukraine War is a single data point in a century-long give and take. It tells us very little. We need a few more years to see what the real impacts — if any — will be. I can only hope that one of the key messages in this book has become clear to you: weapon development is a give and take process. For every introduction of something "new" there is another introduction that takes away the "newness."

INTERIM CONCLUSIONS

The short examples of MBT employment offered above, along with some brief considerations about the future of armour and the current fascination with drone warfare demonstrate five key lessons quite clearly:

1. When tank forces are commanded and employed by those who understand how to do so, the results can be spectacular;
2. Numbers are important but the size of the forces employed is far less decisive than *how* it is employed; and
3. The future is unknowable, but the smart bet is to believe in the historical continuity of conventional arms races. New technology — or the new application of old technology — may seem revolutionary, but it rarely is. There has always been, and as far as we can know, always will be, a give-and-take.

4. The technical capabilities of weapons are important but pale in comparison to the human factors of leadership, skill, tactics, and training.
5. Skill, aggression and smart tactics will overcome technology.

ABOVE: *Insignia of the Drone Battalion of Ukraine's 1st Assault Regiment.*

CONCLUSIONS

The message of this book is straightforward. The tank is *not* obsolete. The Main Battle Tank remains land warfare's single most potent weapon. Although by no means exhaustive, in the process of explaining the message, I covered a great deal of material on modern mechanized warfare that some readers may have found unnecessary. Why? Because there is an enormous amount of uninformed opinion in the media. Therefore, such a broad-based approach was necessary to demonstrate why the tank remains "master" of the modern battlespace.

A literature review of both military journals and open source media demonstrates a consistent trend in the 20th and 21st centuries. There is a tendency on the part of western writers to overvalue technology's role in war making, and the rise of drone warfare, with the mistaken conclusion that the tank is dead, is merely the latest iteration of this unfortunate trend. Why unfortunate? Because it demonstrates an almost wilful insistence on refusing to understand what war is. It is a human endeavour.

Past failures in war have almost always been the result of two fundamental lapses in understanding. First, in not appreciating that the nature of war has never changed. It is today as it was for the Greek hoplites with bronze shields, as it was for Napoleon's Polish cavalry on the western steppes of Russia, as it was for the French behind their Maginot line, and as it is today for Ukrainians in the Donbas. Second, in the misguided belief that technology and not human understanding should guide strategy and tactics. When we combine these two miscalculations, we see a theme. We see a desire to look for technological solutions to human problems, or as one professor once said to me, it seeks to find Roman solutions (engineering) to Greek problems (philosophy).

One message should now be clear. War is at once both science and art. Perhaps more so now than in the past, armoured warfare begins primarily in the realm of science. Further, this science of armoured warfare may originate with the same fundamentals in every country, but as it evolves into an art, social, cultural, and historical impacts affect the employment of all AFVs in general, and of MBTs in particular, differently in every country and in every army. That may seem paradoxical, but it's true. The Russian employment of MBTs is not anything like the British, and the Canadian is not necessarily like the American. This aspect of tank employment is greatly overlooked — even by large segments of professional militaries.

The trigger to the claim of the tank's demise has been the ongoing Russo Ukrainian War. But most of this claim has been based on hyperbole, not fact. In spite of much of the misinformed media hype, the bloody war in Ukraine has not really taught us anything revolutionary about the use of armoured forces (or even drones). It has all been seen before. However, what the claim has done — at least for those with serious intent to learn — is reinforce many of the lessons of the past that have either been ignored, set aside, or simply forgotten.

The continued value of the tank, and the reason that advanced tank design continues around the globe, lies in the tank's unparalleled versatility, survivability, firepower, and its ability to adapt and improve with ever-evolving technologies. Modern tanks feature sophisticated armoured protection systems, which include much more than just adding more layers of steel. New active-armour protection systems enable tanks to operate in high-risk environments in ways that were previously not thought feasible. In the near future, these advances will evolve to counter the drone threat as well, just as every other advancement in the never-ending arms race of tank vs anti-tank has done in the century-long dual between these two battle systems.

There is no question that anti-tank weaponry continues to push technological enhancement of the tank. This deadly cat-and-mouse game speaks to the tank's role in integrating active defensive armour, advanced targeting systems, full-spectrum imaging, and broadband networking, all of which better facilitate both situational awareness, and more important, the building of combat power for commanders and crews at all levels and in all roles. All of these advancements keep tank employment flexible, effective, and fully adaptable to new and growing battlespace challenges.

Mobility, survivability, flexibility, firepower, shock action. All of these characteristics, and more, have always been defining features of tanks, and they continue to be critical for their utility and employment in the battlespace. And they all continue to evolve. But what will these new battlespace challenges bring? We can only make educated guesses, for the future is unknowable. It's clearly evident that technology will continue to be a factor, but here we must be careful.

Recall the example of the Battle of France 1940 and again the Battle for the Golan Heights, both sterling examples where forces with inferior technology and fewer numbers rose to defeat their opponents. But the past does not offer templates or formulae. The past offers only lessons. History, when properly studied, offers perhaps the single greatest warning for modern militaries. Technology always promises more and inevitably delivers less. Technology, in all of its manifestations, is and always has been, an *enabling function* rather than a *deciding function*.

The past not only informs the present; it also educates the present regarding how to prepare for the future. Whatever the future brings to the battlespace — even its abandonment by any forces but drones — one thing is certain: humanity can never disengage itself from this most human of social activities.

Because war is fundamentally a human activity, the last word needs to be about the human in the loop of this ever-evolving cycle of technology-art-employment. We must always remember that war is a human domain and to the extent that it is controllable, it is because *humans* control it. So, if we take away only one solid conclusion from this defence of tanks and armoured warfare, let it be this: No matter how far science advances the technology, the single most important aspect of armoured warfare — or any type of warfare for that matter — remains the crew; the human in the equation. To use the words of Manfred Baron von Richthofen, aviation's infamous "Red Baron", who incidentally began his career as a cavalry officer, "The quality of the crate matters little. Success depends upon the man who sits in it."

ABOVE: The moment that the sabot separates from the armour penetrator of an armour piercing tank round.

ANNEX A: SPLITTING AN MBT SQUADRON

This issue has been a bugbear with me since I was a newly promoted captain and continues to vex me. To my mind it is so basic that I cannot understand why we still make this mistake. I leave it to the readers to make up their own minds.

As I've already said, splitting a squadron of MBTs diminishes its combat power. There are two reasons and here we'll investigate the first, which is that it degrades a key command relationship, which also carries with it the aspect of lessening expertise. To begin, armies where tank companies comprise 10, 12 or 13 tanks don't suffer from this issue. The problem arises with Canadian squadrons which have 19 MBTs per squadron. With four troops of four tanks each and a senior captain who acts as the Squadron Commander's tactical deputy (the Battle Captain), it's easy to fall into the trap of thinking that you can split the squadron into two, two-troop packets, each with a commander.

Here is where it can get confusing. The separation described above (I won't call it splitting) does occur, but you need to understand the specifics to understand when it's an acceptable *separation* and when it's an unacceptable *splitting* of a squadron.

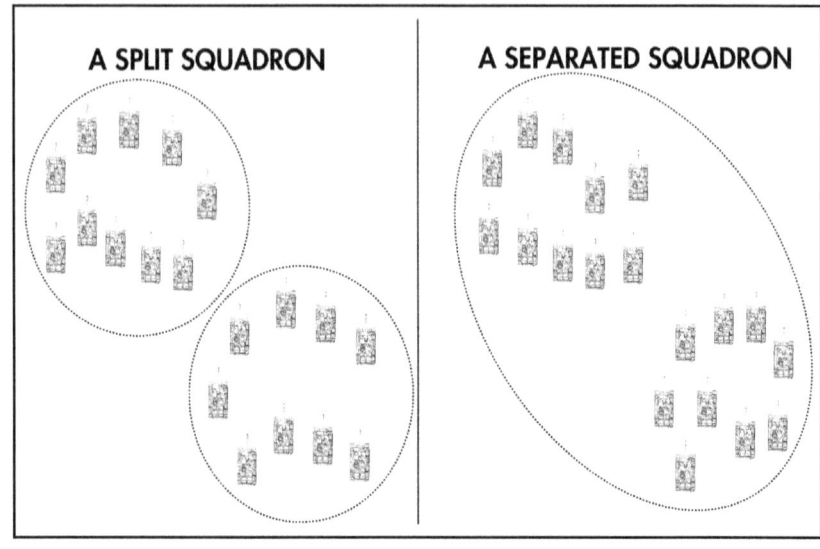

A SPLIT SQUADRON | A SEPARATED SQUADRON

Note: the "Split" MBT sqn is broken into two tactical groupings under two commanders. The dashed lines represent command relationships. The Sqn Minus (10 x MBTs) is commanded by the OC and the Half Sqn by the Battle Captain (BC). Conversely, the "Separated" MBT sqn may indeed be physically spread apart but note the dotted line. The OC continues to command the entire 19 tanks while the BC merely controls the movement of the remaining 9 x MBTs.

If a battlespace is viewed from a helicopter, the two layouts above may indeed look absolutely identical. So, what distinguishes the *unacceptable* from the *acceptable*?

Let's look at each in turn. First let's consider command. The Sqn Commander commands all of the 19 MBTs in her squadron. They may be broken into troops of four for co-ordination purposes, but there is a reason that she is called the Officer Commanding (OC), and her subordinate troops only have troop "leaders". The OC is by definition the most experienced tactical commander in the unit. She is responsible for tactical deployments and solutions to tactical problems as well as everything else that happens under her command.

It's far more than just the legality of "commanding" versus "leading". As the OC, she knows and understands what happens when armour is combined in less than optimal ways and her expertise is the "royal jelly" that differentiates her from other leaders in the unit. So what? So, when attaching MBTs to another combat arm, why would you ignore that expertise? If you split the MBT squadron given to you so that you can evenly distribute tanks among your subordinates, you give up most of the expertise that has been given to you. If an infantry battalion commander does the unthinkable (for me) and gives a tank troop to each of the companies in the unit, the integral combat power of the squadron has been destroyed. Further, the infantry CO has negated the expertise that the MBT OC brought to the unit, thereby diminishing the combat power of the entire battalion.

There are simple ways for the enlightened infantry commander to get both the expertise as well as the maximum combat power. Go back to the diagram of the *separated* squadron. That is the solution.

Let's look at the details. Essentially, you are asking the MBT commander, to separate her troops, and that is *not* a problem because it's normal for MBT commanders to do that — as long as she retains command of all MBTs. It's akin to hiring a plumber to come to your house and when he shows up, you take his tools and make him watch as you plumb your house!

A frequent criticism of my insistence upon never splitting a tank squadron is that MBT OCs actually do it routinely. This critique demonstrates what I also point out above. It may *appear* that the armour commander is splitting her squadron because she has detached one, two, or three tank troops and put the squadron BC in charge for a short-duration task. It's incorrect to see this as splitting because the OC retains command — exercised through her deputy. She can quickly change the disposition of any or all these forces with a simple instruction and the command relationship does not change.

This flexibility of disposition segues nicely to the second reason for never splitting: Logistics. In order to properly explain why logistics is a key issue, let's take a short but important detour away from MBTs and move rearward to the resupply echelons in Annex B.

> **Note:** In Canadian doctrine, splitting a 19-tank MBT squadron is acceptable, as well as a common practice, but that does not make it a sound tactic. Armoured Recce and Armoured Cav squadrons cannot be split.

For non-Canadian readers, the above tendencies are the unfortunate legacy of our army's British heritage and how we fought our tanks during World War II and Korea. Ironically, even the British Army has given up 19-tank squadrons in favour the smaller 13-tank configuration favoured by so many armies. The Canadian habit of splitting our tank forces into smaller component parts continues to baffle many of our allies.

In Canada, as the rest of the world has already done, it's long past time to reevaluate our insistence on such large squadrons in favour of small, more agile configurations. We do not fight the way we did in World War II and modern MBTs are designed to be used much more aggressively than our doctrine disposes us to do.

ABOVE: *Canadian Churchill tanks on Exercise Spartan, conducted in England in March 1943.*

ANNEX B: THE PIG IN THE PYTHON

Note: *The logistics of armoured warfare in general and of tank warfare in particular too often gets short shrift. Visions of battlegroups racing across broad open plains in giant breakthrough battles makes for great cinematography, but the reality is far more mundane. All armoured warfare demands vast amounts of logistic support and commanders who are loathe to learn this fundamental lesson are doomed to failure. If they are lucky, like the Commander of a German tank brigade for whom I worked, the worst they get is a scolding from the Division Commander. If they are unlucky, they could doom their command to catastrophic defeat.*

Let's consider logistics at the most basic level for a tank commander — an MBT squadron equipped with a generic MBT that has a 1,000 litre fuel capacity. In an MBT squadron on operations, the Squadron Sergeant-Major (SSM) follows the squadron one or two tactical bounds back and monitors the battle. Let's say that he knows that most tanks have used up about 50 litres of fuel so he asks the OC if he can move up to refuel the rear troops as the squadron moves forward. Only those MBTs out of contact will refuel. It's a well-rehearsed drill.

You might wonder, why bother taking on 50 litres of fuel? After all, more than 900 litres are still on board each tank, which could travel another couple of days. (We'll keep it simple with round numbers.)

Let's do the arithmetic. The tanks now have approximately 19,000 litres of total fuel. As well, the SSM has two fuel trucks with 10,000 litres each for a total of another 20,000 litres. If he pushes 50 litres of fuel to each tank each time he can (let's say four times a day for argument's sake), he will empty one truck in approximately two and a half days (50 x 4 x 19 x 2.5= 9,500). That leaves him with a full tanker to keep pushing fuel while the empty one runs back to the brigade area to top up. Now imagine that for some reason, the tank regiment is in pursuit, or some other complex operation and the CO decides to run the risk and *not* allow the squadron echelons to push fuel because it will slow down the advance. With three identical squadrons and assuming that everyone started fully fuelled, the CO has less than five days to fight the enemy (4 x 50 = 200 litres/tank/day). At that point the MBTs will all be bone dry.

Then what? For starters, like it or not, the three tank SSMs in the unit must come forward and empty their fuel trucks *at the same time*. The CO has put himself in a perilous spot. What if the tanks are still pursuing? What if the regiment is in the midst of an engagement? The CO has no choice. Tanks without fuel are just targets. Even if the tanks manage to start refuelling, the CO has created an enormous headache for all support personnel (and commanders) — not just in each of the squadrons but in the brigade *and* the division.

All six regimental tank fuel trucks (two per squadron) will have to begin shuttling back and forth to the rear echelons and draw 60,000 litres of fuel. In the meantime, the tank regiment continues to use fuel all the while running the risk of being nothing more than the world's most expensive set of paperweights! Even *if* the brigade can give him the fuel he wants, which is *highly* unlikely, he has forced every squadron OC and troop leader to stop and wait their turn for the fuel trucks to replenish their tanks. It's court martial time …

The problems that the CO has created by not allowing subordinate commanders to constantly replenish are both logistical and tactical. By stopping the trickle of fuel (and assuming a running battle, the same is true for ammunition) the CO has inadvertently created the proverbial "pig in the python". The brigade (python) will be unable to swallow the enormous amount of supply (pig) that will be needed all at once. As a result, it will take days and many sleepless nights of fuel vehicles shuttling back and forth to once again allow the system to correct itself. But that is only half the problem. There are tactical issues as well.

The logistics of pushing fuel (and ammunition) forward is like a conveyor belt, only more complex. Not only must supplies constantly be brought forward, but there also needs to be a bit of elasticity in the conveyor belt so that surges in demand, or a sudden lack of demand, can be accommodated. Remember that fighting formations only have limited storage capacity. In conventional warfare, these formations are constantly on the move. In order for the system to work effectively, fuel and other supplies must always be available but never become a burden or a liability. For MBTs, one of the ways that we ensure this balance is to constantly take on fuel and ammunition, even when we already have what we consider to be an ample supply.

If tactical units are unable to move or shoot, they are not effective tools for the commanders to build combat power. They are just the opposite; they are liabilities. In the extreme situation above, the CO's desire to maintain high-speed operations has put not only the unit's own soldiers at risk, but those of superior commanders as well. The tank regiment is integral to building combat power. Should it suddenly run out of fuel it's worse than useless because the unit will drain resources away from other units to get quickly back up to operating capacity. This makes the regiment a combat *diminisher* rather than the reverse.

Sound like an improbable situation? In 1987, as the personal assistant to the commander of the *Bundeswehr 10. Panzerbrigade* I watched an entire Leopard II battalion run out of fuel on a major field training exercise for the reasons I just described. Decades of peacetime training limitations caused the *Bundeswehr* to lose its understanding of logistic requirements of long-range armour deployments. My commander ordered a 125 km counter-attack, and no one planned for the fuel. This was skill fade in an army that had once moved armoured corps from the Atlantic Ocean to the Ural Mountains.

No senior armoured commander would willingly deny subordinate tank commanders fuel. But that is not to say that there might be a tactical situation where a similar condition could arise. A squadron might inadvertently outpace its supply echelons (as did General Patton in France). Whatever the scenario, all armour commanders at all levels need to understand what happens when the resupply conveyor belt is disrupted.

Back to our squadron OC in an infantry battalion. Even if the gaining infantry commander appreciates this logistics dilemma, he may not understand that splitting the MBT squadron effectively ties the hands of both the SSM and the squadron OC. Recall that the squadron's supply echelons have two ammo carriers and two fuel carriers. By pairing them, the SSM keeps supplies flowing from the rear echelons to just behind the squadron and to the fighters. If the squadron is split, it takes one ammo carrier and one fuel carrier for each half. Now the SSM is crippled. He cannot keep the *pig* moving in the *python*. But if the squadron is simply separated, the OC has the skill, along with the SSM, to keep everything flowing as it should.

Why would any commander *intentionally* diminish combat power?

CONCLUSION: *Never* split MBT squadrons. Tell the OC what you want. Then let *them* do it. (*Auftragstaktik*)

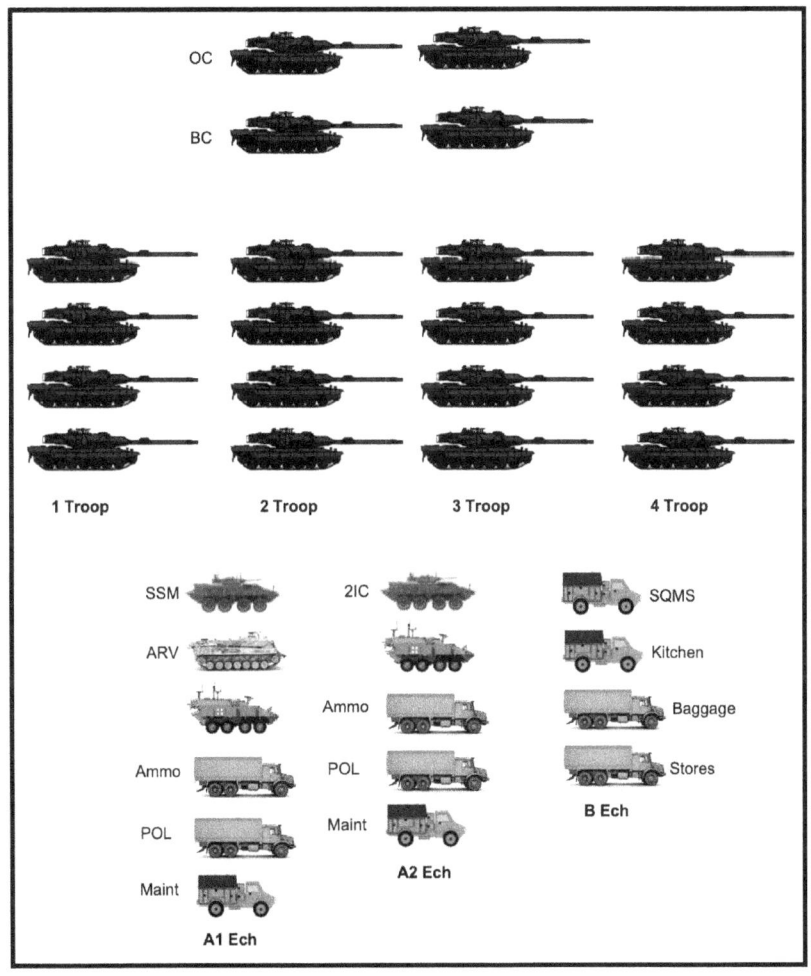

ABOVE: *Organization of a typical Canadian tank squadron, including its echelon.*

ANNEX C: PEELING THE ONION

Note: The explanation below is highly simplified for the general reader. Properly placing, and effectively fighting a combined arms team in a defensive position takes years of training and experience. It isn't for the faint of heart.

We have covered many subjects from how tanks are designed, to what distinguishes an MBT from a generic tank to the notion of combat power and even touched upon combined arms theory. All of this was in aid of appreciating how important the modern MBT really is. Now, we will use a specific type of battle to put together all of these points. We'll look at how using a combined arms team in the defence can avert a combined arms attack that is multiple times the size of the defending force. The key to understanding this analysis lies in appreciating one critical premise: each of the experts that made up the combined arms team was free to use his or her expertise to maximum advantage and not hampered by a commander who insisted on controlling every aspect of every weapon system.

Generally, when establishing a defensive position, the commander needs to think of destroying the attacker like peeling an onion. In other words, strip away combat power in a layered, predetermined way. The defender must assume that the attacker has done everything possible to maximize combat power for the assault. He will not attack randomly. Therefore, removing the attacker's strength randomly will only ensure that the enemy hits your position with most of his combat power intact. Let's look at why.

The skilled attacker layers the attack to maximize the shock. The smart defender layers the defence by weapon effect and by range bands in order to dissipate the attacker's combat power. The reality of the defence is that to completely repel the attacker indefinitely is unrealistic. At some point the attacker will break in, so the defender needs to make the cost of doing so unacceptably high, even to the point of allowing penetration in order to kill at close range.

How does the defender make it "expensive"? Shape where the break-in will be. To do this, the defender sites weapon systems to overlap each other, to canalize the enemy into killing zones and to gain synergistic effects. Step one is to site the longest-ranged direct fire weapons. These may be MBTs, or they may be Anti-Armour weapons. Siting them first ensures that their mobility is not hampered. Next, the weapons with the next-longest ranges will be sited and so on.

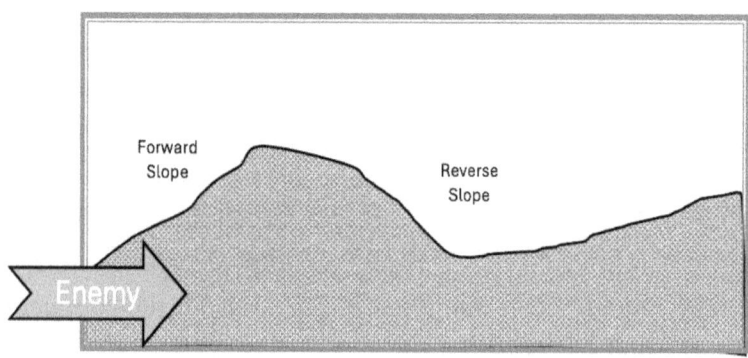

These two will work together to ensure that they optimize their ability to strip away the key enemy vehicles. Once this is done, the infantry is positioned for mutual support and to provide close protection to the long-range weapons. If possible, the infantry will be placed on a reverse slope (protected on the back side of the hill) making them invisible to assaulting forces).

Siting a combined arms defence is no small task, even at the company combat team level, and will take a great deal of time and effort. Here the infantry commander must strike a balance. She must trust her subordinates to place their systems where they will give her the most combat power while also restricting them from placing their weapons where they will impinge upon the effects of the others. She must trust the individual commanders to do their jobs, but at this level the individual platoon, troop or detachment commanders will not have as much understanding of the combined-arms battle as the OC. Therefore, before her position is considered combat ready, she will inspect all of the weapon emplacements, walk the whole position with her Company Sergeant-Major (CSM) and her respective subordinate commanders, and make any necessary adjustments.

Time to "peel the onion". We won't discuss the minefields or artillery fire plans, and assume that our combat engineer and artillery commanders have done their level best.

How will our combat team commander fight this battle? She'll place strength against weakness — even when it's counter-intuitive, like not allowing tanks to shoot at other tanks! Again, let's make some assumptions for the sake of simplicity. The attacker will have at least *three times* the force as the defender and will assault just as we would. Our notional OC, is part of a battalion defence, which will be part of a brigade defence. In front of her, there would have been several levels of Armoured Cav, and Armoured Recce forces as part of the Covering Force, both controlled by senior HQs. The covering force battle has been fought, the Recce and Cav have done their jobs and have been withdrawn through her position into depth. No friendly forces remain between the combat team and the enemy assault forces.

As the enemy force approaches, the defenders know that their success hinges on one key effect: They must separate the attacker's

MBTs from his infantry. If those two arms strike in harmony, then defence becomes almost impossible. Enemy Armoured Recce must be stripped away to blind the oncoming commander. If they are light reconnaissance, the OC will use artillery to destroy them. If they are Armoured Cav, she will use her Anti-Armour platoon, which will have been tracking all tanks leading the assault. Once they enter the optimum range band, the Anti-Armour platoon commander will open with a volley that will attempt to wipe away all the leading MBTs with one swipe. No doubt, enemy artillery has already begun to strike our position, so life is getting precarious for both sides about now.

It's time to discuss briefly the priority of targets and sequencing of fire. Think of the classic British "thin red line". This formation usually consisted of a battalion arrayed in two rows, one standing while the other knelt. The standing line would hold fire until almost point-blank range, fire on command, and then kneel to re-load. The kneeling rank would immediately stand and on order do the same. The effect on attacking troops was devastating as successive walls of lead struck them every few seconds. A well-trained battalion could literally stop an attack in its tracks.

In our modern age, it's difficult to imagine the savage carnage of the 19th century battlefield. The only hope for survival in many of those bloodlettings was iron discipline. The side that broke ranks first inevitably was cut to pieces by cavalry. Although not much from 19th century linear tactics survives into our day, the concept of such highly disciplined and coordinated firepower does.

Our Combat Team OC cannot allow subordinates to fire at will at anything they like. Neither can she assign targets to individual weapons as the enemy approaches. What she does instead is create a firing priority and a methodology that allows her to control the "wall of lead" that she sends against the attacker. Based on all of the battlespace variables she has been juggling, the OC will issue orders telling the various subordinate commanders what to shoot at and when. For instance, it's common that everyone will be on the lookout for fighting vehicles with multiple antenna arrays. These are invariably command and control vehicles (commanders, artillery, and Armoured Recce HQs) and killing them early will help raise the level of friction and chaos in the attacking force.

Next, the OC will decide whether she wants to strip the MBTs from their supporting infantry or vice versa. This will depend on several factors including those already mentioned. Either, once determined, the early shooting will be at these targets almost exclusively. This is where the range bands come into play and the priorities may well change as the ranges become shorter.

Let's look at one specific weapon, the MBT (my favourite). The high precision and rapid fire of tank gunnery plays a key role in creating the synergy that our OC seeks. All the MBTs will have been tracking all of the infantry vehicles seeking protection behind the advancing armour. If Anti-Armour has done its work, most of those MBTs are now stopped, on fire, or destroyed, and they will withdraw to the rear. Here is the point where it becomes controversial. On order from the MBT commander, all friendly tanks open fire at once — but *not* at the remaining MBTs. They fire at the infantry fighting vehicles (IFVs). The effect of this volley fire on the assault should be like hitting a wall.

The MBTs should fire armour piercing shot (APFSDS) at the infantry – not because they need it to pierce their vehicles, but because these rounds are hypersonic and 100% lethal. The accuracy of such shooting is in the high 90% and every infantry vehicle struck kills or wounds an entire enemy section/squad. One round; eight to ten dead. Timing is critical. The MBTs need to allow the attacking infantry to come close enough to ensure quick first-round kills, but not so close that they will consider dismounting and approaching on foot. Either way, having done their deadly duty, the tanks will quickly move out of their firing positions and join the Anti-Armour in the rear to await the next phase. But if all of the commanders have done their jobs well, it has been a very bad day for the enemy and the next phase will be to attend to the wounded, remove damaged vehicles and prepare to do it again against a fresh enemy. The combined arms attack has had its cohesion ripped to pieces and the attack is likely over.

Whether the firing priority was MBT or IFV, once half the attacking combined arms team has been stripped away, the attack is over. Remember, MBTs are vulnerable without supporting infantry and IFVs are vulnerable without supporting MBTs.

Let's review and summarize. If the above description seems simple and mechanical, then you need to re-read and re-consider. It's anything but. The sequence described above is highly complex with literally thousands of points where friction can reduce the whole process to a disorderly mess. Such "peeling" requires high levels of leadership, control, discipline and initiative (exactly as described in my short volume, *Tactical Jazz*). Further, what I've described above is a highly simplified version of reality but is purposely so to be instructive. If we were having the same discussion with experienced tacticians we would have spent much more time considering such details as the various forms of enemy recce, the effects of enemy artillery, where the enemy Main Effort was (if we could find it), how we should emplace our engineer obstacles to canalize the attacker and dozens of other specifics that junior commanders only come to appreciate with practice and experience.

So, why the "peel" methodology? Because it's the best option to counter the effects of the enemy's combined arms synergy. Consider these scenarios: a combined arms enemy force is stripped of all of its armour during the assault. Will it dismount and assault on foot for over a kilometer in the face of a dug-in defender? Unlikely. What about the reverse? What if we allow the MBTs to approach unscathed but remove all of the supporting infantry? Will these MBTs assault a dug-in position? Most assuredly not. MBTs without close support infantry should never attack dug-in infantry. It's suicidal. The only chance of success in the mechanized battlespace is with a combined arms team. Destroy the cohesion of that team and its combat power will be diminished such that it becomes an unviable force. Once again, we are back to the idea that we must always consider our tactics based on the building and the destroying of combat power. Coordinating your own combat power in order to destroy an enemy's combat power is neither easy nor simple. Experience, judgement, and a myriad of other factors — like the correct employment of armour — are the keys to success.

OTHER BOOKS BY COLONEL C.S. OLIVIERO

DANGEROUS LESSONS

THE TRUTH IS THAT ARMIES RARELY TEACH TACTICS.

They drill procedures, rehearse checklists, and memorize doctrine — but the art of thinking and fighting, the essence of command, is left to chance. The result is predictable: leaders who can pass an exam but falter when lives depend on their judgment.

Dangerous Lessons is a guide to breaking that cycle. It strips away the false comfort of rote answers and gives leaders the means to actually teach tactics — with all the risk-taking, creativity, and focus that requires.

Inside, you'll learn how to:

- Train decision-makers, not box-tickers.
- Kill false lessons in training—before they kill soldiers in combat.
- Use mistakes to build skill, not to break confidence.
- Turn the chaos of battle to your own advantage.

Poorly designed training leads to bad habits, and bad habits get soldiers killed. *Dangerous Lessons* shows leaders how to build training that forges judgment, initiative, and resilience — the real weapons of war. The best welfare for soldiers is good, realistic training.

Dangerous Lessons shows you how to give them nothing less.

OTHER BOOKS BY COLONEL C.S. OLIVIERO | 119

TACTICAL JAZZ

CHARLES S. OLIVIERO

AUTHOR OF PRAXIS TACTICUM, STRATEGIA AND AUFTRAGSTAKTIK

TACTICAL JAZZ

TRUST, ADAPT AND IMPROVISE

Books on leadership too often read like manufacturer's assembly manuals: Insert Tab A into Slot B, and so on. *Tactical Jazz* provides a uniquely different approach. It casts ideas at the reader as pebbles are dropped into a pond.

With the narrative finesse of a storyteller and the insight of a strategist, Colonel Oliviero invites readers to reconsider the tenets of leadership through the lens of creativity. Like a jazz combo, great teams thrive when individuals master their roles and synchronize instinctively, adapting to the rhythm of uncertainty.

Whether you're commanding troops, leading a business conglomerate, or beginning a tech start-up, *o*presents practical wisdom to foster initiative, build trust, and create synergy. Filled with vivid anecdotes, transformative concepts, and a touch of Zen philosophy, this book furnishes leaders and managers, at every level, the tools to cultivate resilience, innovation, and unity of purpose.

In leadership, as in jazz, success is not found in following a score — success is found in creating something extraordinary together.

Auftragstaktik

✠ The Birth of Enlightened Leadership ✠

The Author of Praxis Tacticum and Strategia

Colonel Charles S. Oliviero

AUFTRAGSTAKTIK
The Birth of Enlightened Leadership

Auftragstaktik (mission-type tactics) were the foundation of Prussia's, and later Germany's, astounding battlefield performances. Universally praised in military circles, *Auftragstaktik* remains both poorly understood and badly practised. It is sometimes mistaken to be a military leadership strategy, when in fact it is a philosophy that applies to the exercise of leadership in nearly any situation. For many reasons, this uniquely German approach to leadership lies shrouded in a fog of mystery and misinterpretation.

Colonel Oliviero clears away that fog.

He concisely explains the early intellectual and structural growth of this leadership philosophy from before the French Revolution to the eve of the First World War, with a glimpse at the interwar period. He provides the necessary background and understanding to any reader, military or civilian, looking to learn about using mission-type tactics through the lens of history.

STRATEGIA

A PRIMER ON THEORY AND STRATEGY
FOR STUDENTS OF WAR

COLONEL CHARLES S. OLIVIERO

STRATEGIA
A Primer on Theory and Strategy for Students of War

War fascinates us, but what do we really know about its nature?

Strategia is the product of Colonel Oliviero's decades-long intellectual quest to address this fundamental query. His work offers both the serious student and the casual reader a foundation stone upon which to build a deeper understanding of military thought and theory, and thereby a richer appreciation of mankind's deadliest pursuit.

Strategia introduces many of the major contributors to military thought and theory as well as some of their most profound impacts on the conduct of war, from Sun-Tzu to the modern day, encompassing warfare on land, at sea and in the air, as well as in the cyber-realm.

While not an all-encompassing deep dive, *Strategia* is an essential primer and a point of departure. With this foundation stone in place, the student of war can proceed to follow Clausewitz's admonition to develop a "fine and penetrating mind."

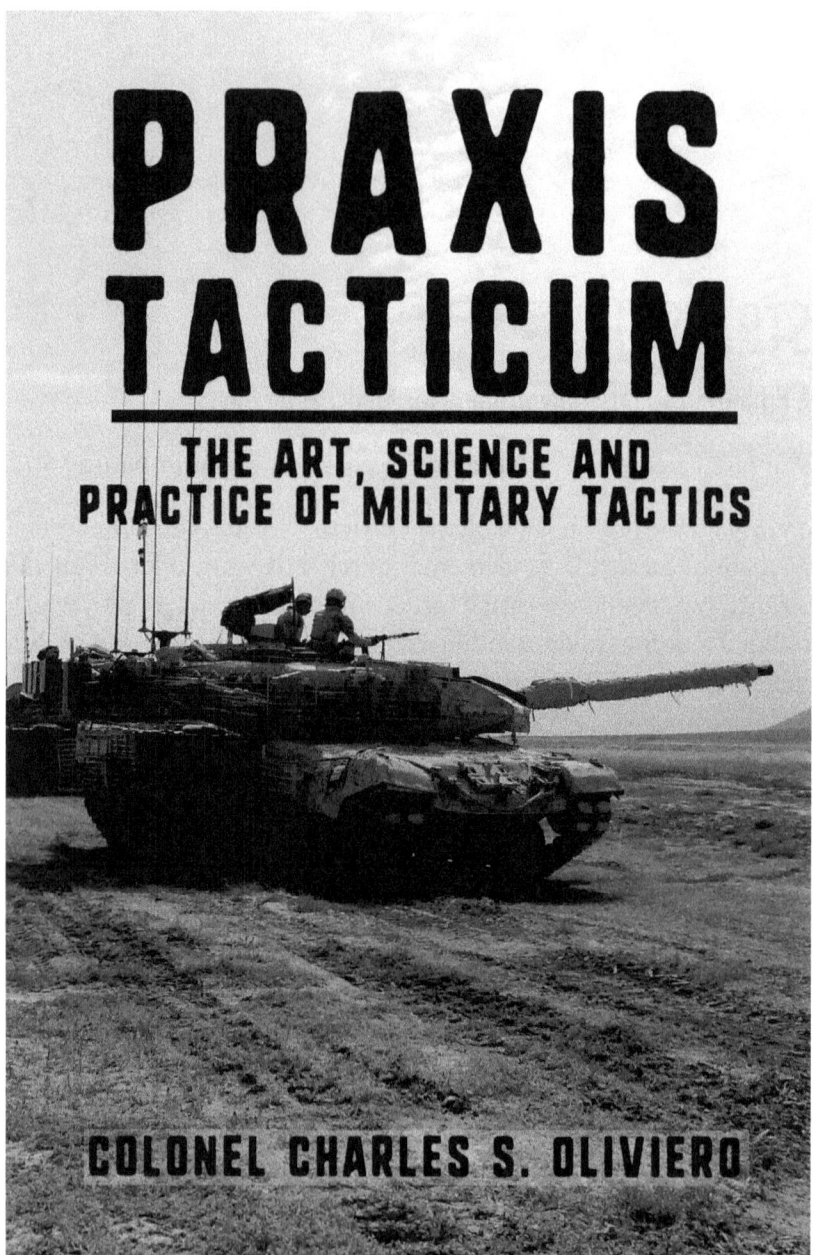

PRAXIS TACTICUM

TACTICUM

THE ART, SCIENCE AND
PRACTICE OF MILITARY TACTICS

COLONEL CHARLES S. OLIVIERO

PRAXIS TACTICUM
The Art, Science and Practice of Military Tactics

Pundits have long predicted the end of conventional warfare but for the foreseeable future, it is here to stay. Counterinsurgency, guerrilla warfare, terrorism, peace enforcement, policing.

All these forms, like conventional warfare, are as old as mankind. Modern militaries claim to be professional bodies, responsible for the education, control and discipline of their members. But at least one aspect of this claim is poorly executed: tactics are not taught to junior leaders, which is why this guide is essential reading for all junior leaders, officers and NCOs alike.

There is a military adage that there is no teacher like the enemy. True; but the wise commander prepares to meet that enemy and become their teacher instead. This is your essential study guide.

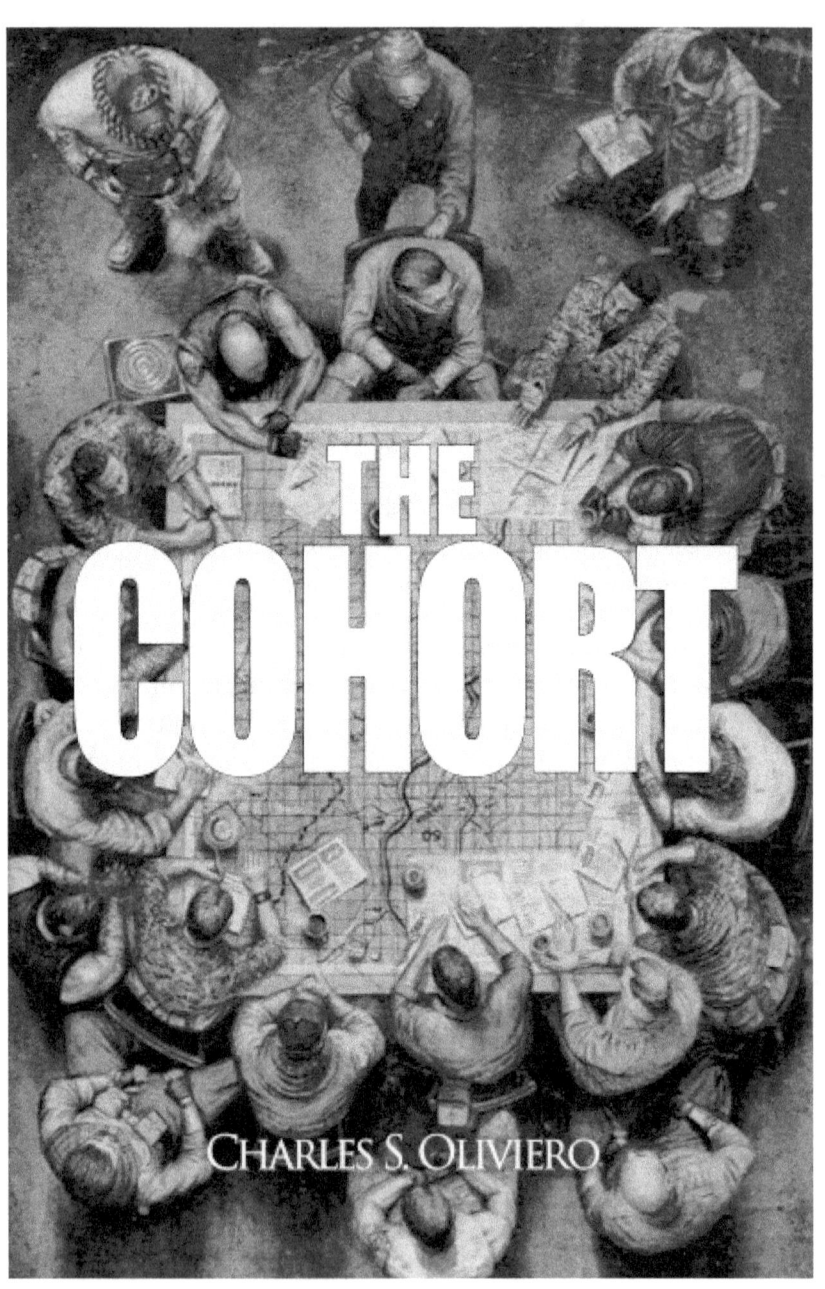

THE COHORT

Though slated for high command, Colonel Amadeus Ignazio "Skip" Schiaparelli abandoned his life in uniform when the Army no longer felt like home. Retiring to a contemplative existence in Italy, he is recruited by an American intelligence officer with a stirring proposal. Intrigued, if somewhat skeptical, Skip accepts the offer and is thereafter launched into a shadowy world of lies and deception which threaten many of his core beliefs.

Skip is a man committed to the ancient principles imparted to him by his father: trust, friendship and honour. He surrounds himself with friends, both old and new, who share those same beliefs. But even in Eden there was a snake, and betrayal threatens this new life of brotherhood and fraternal fidelity that he creates.

Whatever the challenge, Skip follows his guiding principle, that trust is earned not given. But in a world of deception, can one man trust his own instincts?

ACKNOWLEDGEMENTS

Once more, I would like to thank my old friend and high school mate, Angelo Mattachione for prompting me to pen this book, Professor James Boutilier for graciously agreeing to write the Preface as well as my friend, editor, and publisher Phil Halton for pushing me to write it. It's good to have friends.

I would also like to thank my group of so-called Beta Readers for their time and their valuable comments and insights as well as those who took the time to offer their opinions in print.

ABOUT THE AUTHOR

Colonel Chuck Oliviero, PhD spent almost four decades in the Canadian Army as an Armoured Cavalry officer. He spent half of his career either as a student or as a teacher and the other half commanding troops. He is the author of four non-fiction books on war and strategy: *Praxis Tacticum*, *Strategia*, *Auftragstaktik* and *Dangerous Lessons*, as well as one novel, *The Cohort*. All are published by Double Dagger Books and available worldwide.

DOUBLE DAGGER BOOKS

Conflict and warfare have shaped human history since before we began to record it. The earliest stories that we know of, passed on as oral tradition, speak of war, and more importantly, the essential elements of the human condition that are revealed under its pressure.

We are dedicated to publishing material that, while rooted in conflict, transcend the idea of "war" as merely a genre. Fiction, non-fiction, and stuff that defies categorization, we want to read it all.

Because if you want peace, study war.

www.ingramcontent.com/pod-product-compliance
Lightning Source LLC
Chambersburg PA
CBHW061805120626
46550CB00005B/2146